Focus on the Family®

Christian Heritage TEACHING GUIDE

The Santa Fe Years

Nancy Rue

BETHANY HOUSE PUBLISHERS
MINNEAPOLIS, MINNESOTA 55438

Christian Heritage Series Teaching Guide, The Santa Fe Years

Cover design by Sheryl Thornberg
Interior design by Sherry Paavola

The author is represented by the literary agency of Alive Communications, 7680 Goddard, Colorado Springs, CO 80920.

Published by Bethany House Publishers
A Ministry of Bethany Fellowship International
11300 Hampshire Avenue South
Minneapolis, Minnesota 55438
www.bethanyhouse.com

Printed in the United States of America by
Bethany Press International, Minneapolis, Minnesota 55438

ISBN: 1-56179-897-5

Unless otherwise indicated, Scripture quotations are taken from the *King James Version*.

Focus on the Family books are available at special quantity discounts when purchased in bulk by corporations, organizations, churches, or groups. Special imprints, messages, and excerpts can be produced to meet your needs. For more information, contact: Resource Sales Group, Focus on the Family, 8605 Explorer Drive, Colorado Springs, CO 80920; or phone (800) 932-9123.

Printed in the United States of America
1 2 3 4 5 6 7 8 9 / 08 07 06 05 04 03 02

Contents

Teacher to Teacher

Whether you have 35 desks in your classroom or two chairs pulled up to the dining room table, you have a valuable job to do. I know—I've been in your shoes. I've done more teaching than just about anything else, including writing and driving my little green Volkswagen Beetle with Country and Western music blaring (my other lifelong loves). I've spent 16 years teaching in public schools, five years leading creative dramatics workshops, 22 years mentoring my budding-author daughter, and five years teaching writing workshops for "kids" of all ages—all the while tutoring potential young authors one-on-one. My entire adult life has been spent sharing what I know with kids and learning with them as we explore, discover, and create.

I've learned two important things from those years in education (besides never to turn my back on a kid who looks angelically innocent):

1. Teaching is hard work.
2. Teachers need all the help we can get, no matter how good at it we already are.

Unfortunately, most of us educators are usually so swamped that we don't have time to even think about sharing the materials we *have* had a chance to discover. That's why I've developed this teaching guide to accompany The Christian Heritage Series. It's my way of propping open my classroom door and pulling out my idea files for you to dig through.

Inside you'll find materials designed for kids from third to eighth grades. I hope you'll be able to use them, whether you're teaching public school kids, Christian school students, or your own offspring. The guide is organized as follows:

History Folder: Gives a quick rundown on the historical background for The Santa Fe Years and activities for tying *The Discovery, The Mirage, The Stand, The Mission, The Struggle,* and *The Choice* into your study of American history.

Literature Folder: An explanation of a basic element of literature illustrated in each book, with suggested activities for reinforcing the concepts. These are continued from the guides for The Salem Years, The Williamsburg Years, The Charleston Years, and The Chicago Years, but can be used effectively even if this is your first use of The Christian Heritage Series.

Writing Folder: Ideas for getting pens into hands. These activities key into the books' themes and the ways they relate to the lives of today's children. They're presented in skill-building order.

Christianity Folder: Ways in which the books can be used by public school teachers as a history of religion in America and as support for basic value study, and by Christian school teachers and homeschooling parents as illustrations of people living (or not living) their Christian principles.

Ways-to-Make-It-Matter Folder: A file of projects students can do at the end of the six-book series to pull together what they've learned about literature, history, themselves, and God. The ideas can be used "as is" or lead to just-perfect projects you and your kids design together.

Feel-Free-to-Photocopy Folder: Reproducible activity sheets on three levels (third/fourth grades, fifth/sixth grades, seventh/eighth grades). These sheets are referred to in the other sections of the book, advising when and how to use them.

History Folder

Note: In the **Feel-Free-to-Photocopy Folder**, there is a history sheet for each book for each grade level, to be used in addition to or instead of the activity given for each book here in the **History Folder**. This gives you options, depending on how much time you want to spend on each book and area.

The Discovery

It is the spring of 1944 when The Santa Fe Years begin. America has been engaged in the Second World War since December 7, 1941, when the Japanese attacked the U.S. base at Pearl Harbor, Hawaii, destroying seven battleships, eight other vessels, and 188 aircraft, and killing 2,403 Americans. It was a day that President Franklin D. Roosevelt said would "live in infamy."

The war itself had been going on in Europe since 1938, when Adolph Hitler, the German dictator, seized Austria and began a campaign against the Jews with Kristallnacht, a vicious and calculated strategy to destroy all Jewish businesses within the Nazi realm.

Following the Nazi doctrine which Hitler espoused, he and his allies were basically attempting to take over the world and to "cleanse" it ethnically, as evidenced by Mussolini beginning his fascist reign in Italy, and Japan in its brutal, genocidal war against China. Germany, Italy, and Japan became known as the Axis Powers, a term that loosely tied them together in their view of world power.

Before December 7, 1941, there had been much debate in the United States over whether America should become involved in the war. Hitler continued to claim that each territory he took would be his "last territorial demand in Europe." But he bluffed his way into slowly taking over Europe and its natural resources until the threat of his dictatorship becoming even more widespread was alarmingly apparent.

The attack on Pearl Harbor galvanized the nation and made a declaration of war on Japan unavoidable. Then, on December 10, 1941, Germany and Italy, united by the Axis Powers agreement, declared war on the United States.

Oil was the driving force behind Japan's attack on America. The islands in the Pacific provided shipping lanes to oil for Japan, and so the Japanese had begun to take them over, inspired by Hitler's success in Europe so far. Crippling American military power was vital if Japan was going to be successful in keeping the Pacific islands in its hands.

The American government was aware of that, and as early as 1939, the U.S. military began anti-aircraft training in preparation for conflict in the Pacific. The 1,841 New Mexicans who made up the 200th Coast Artillery—of which our fictitious character Rudy Hutchinson, Will's father, is a part—were one of the groups involved in such training, beginning on January 6, 1941. In August, the 200th was selected by the War Department for service in the Philippine Islands because of its advanced state of training, and by November its troops were ready to defend Fort Stotsenburg (near Manila) from possible Japanese attack.

On December 8, 1941, the day after the Japanese attack on Pearl Harbor, Fort Stotsenburg was also bombed, but the 200th was able to hold fast until December 24, 1941, when Japanese ground forces entered the scene. By December 31, the 200th had shot down 23 Japanese bombers, but the presence of ground troops forced the 200th to gradually withdraw, until by April, even though they had brought down 86 Japanese airplanes, the anti-aircraft equipment had to be destroyed to prevent its capture by the Japanese.

Shortly after noon on April 9, 1942, Japanese officers arrived at Bataan Field, where the 200th was waiting for food and medical supplies, and forced the surrender of New Mexico's anti-aircraftsmen—as well as the other American and Filipino soldiers fighting at their sides—and made them prisoners.

Six days after the surrender, the 76,000 soldiers, sick and starving, were herded off on a 60-mile forced march, an ordeal during which many of their Japanese guards proved murderously sadistic. The Japanese warrior code—*bushido*—viewed soldiers who surrendered as beneath contempt, so prisoners who fell out of the march, exhausted, were bayoneted or shot to death. Thirst-crazed men who drank from roadside ditches were beaten or killed. Prisoners with dysentery who stopped to relieve themselves were shot. At the San Fernando railhead, the remaining prisoners were jammed into unventilated boxcars and transported northward. Those who survived that trip then had to make a final seven-mile march, under the tropical sun, to a prison camp. Ten thousand prisoners (2,000 of them Americans) died on the Bataan Death March. The enemy's capacity for inhumanity shocked the American people and aroused their determination to destroy the Japanese empire.

Armed with that hatred, many Americans thought that the war with Japan would be short-lived. Those small, strange-looking, backward Japanese, they said, weren't capable of competing physically or technologically with the Americans. But early in the war, Japan enjoyed overwhelming military superiority in the Pacific, winning victory after victory, beginning in Guam. America's lack of experience in air combat was also a problem, since Japan had already fought China in the air and had the advantage of previous knowledge. By the spring of 1942, Japan ruled most of the Pacific Ocean, all the way down to the doorstep of Australia. Its purpose was to maintain control of the raw materials (such as the oil we've already mentioned) which Japan itself could not produce, so it was the job of the American military and her allies to slash the ability of the Japanese to produce military goods and equipment, while we continued to produce better planes, ships, and military hardware. Fortunately, the attack on Pearl Harbor had not damaged repair shops, power plants, or gasoline tanks, and 70 of the fleet's vessels and three aircraft carriers were not in the harbor at the time.

Until the summer of 1942, President Roosevelt felt that until the European war could be won against Nazi Germany, the Japanese should merely be kept from advancing too far. But military commanders knew the tide had to be turned before the Japanese owned every piece of land from China to Australia, and they knew our country's morale needed a boost. The tide did begin to turn when one of the most decisive battles of the war, Midway Island, was fought.

Midway was a small but strategic island northwest of Hawaii, where the Japanese lost more than 300 planes in two days. Four of the Japanese Navy's nine aircraft carriers were sunk in the fighting, and this loss erased Japan's military advantage on the sea. Japanese industry couldn't rebuild in time to stand up to the growing U.S. power, and never again did the Japanese have the firepower to range at will across the Pacific theater.

By November of 1943, the U.S. was able to begin "island-hopping" through the Central Pacific, taking one by one the islands Japan had managed to capture. The U.S. strategy (put simply for those of us whose minds are easily boggled by such things!) was to ferry ground troops to an island. When that island was captured, the U.S. would use it as an air and supply base for attacking the next island up the line. This would drive the Japanese farther and farther from their own bases, making it more and more difficult for them to get their ground troops in.

It would be helpful, in explaining this background to students, to have a map of the Pacific and to point out the "necklace" of islands we're talking about. The first target was the Gilbert Islands, starting with the Tarawa Atoll (an atoll being a circle of tiny islands). Next they moved to the Marshall Islands in January 1944, a little over two years after the attack on Pearl Harbor—which shows what a slow, laborious process it was. When the Marshall Islands were taken, the U.S. moved on to the Mariana Islands, halfway between the Gilberts and Japan, which they had to take in order to be able to attack the Japanese mainland. By now, the U.S. Navy had a wealth of experienced air crew and aircraft, and at that point, most of the Japanese air crews were novice replacements.

This is where Book 1, *The Discovery*, begins—a time when the U.S. began to see hope, but saw the unwillingness of the Japanese to surrender as well.

The Second World War was truly a *world* war, and at the time our story opens there seemed to be no place on earth that wasn't in the throes of the hideous conflict—the South Pacific, Europe, the Indian Ocean, the Far East, East Asia, the Atlantic Ocean, Russia, North Africa, the Middle East. It probably isn't necessary for any student in grades 3 through 8 to know every single battle that occurred, but it is important for them to realize just how widespread the tragedy was. Just a few facts might help you to get that across.

- The Allies were the United States, Great Britain (which had so far been inspiring in its doggedness and valor), and Russia (which Germany had invaded in June of 1941 and where Stalin was building up a Soviet army). President Roosevelt and Britain's Prime Minister Winston Churchill became the spokesmen for freedom.
- The Axis powers, the enemies of the Allies, were Germany, Italy, and Japan. They wanted to rule the world within 10 years.
- The war was fought in what became known as two theaters—the European theater and the Pacific theater. They're also referred to at times as *fronts*.
- By 1940, France (where German troops controlled Paris), Belgium, the Netherlands, Luxembourg, Denmark, Norway, and Romania had all fallen to the Nazis.
- Little progress was being made by the Allies in Europe.

Home-Front Details in *The Discovery*

What was happening on the U.S. home front was extremely important. Although the war was not physically being fought on U.S. land, Americans were profoundly affected, and the World War II generation developed a strong commitment to family values and community. Many people only in their twenties showed maturity beyond their years. The kinds of things they had to cope with which are featured in Book 1 are: food rationing with ration coupons; the complete lack of things like nylon for stockings, rubber for tires, and metal for new cars; war stamps and war bonds; censored mail; kids growing up without their dads; moms working outside the home, many of them for the first time; Victory Gardens; telegrams; the draft (Selective Service); gas rationing; air-raid drills.

Ethnic Details in *The Discovery*

Because Santa Fe, the setting for the books, is populated by Hispanics, Indians (called that before it became politically correct to call them Native Americans), and Anglos (whites), students will learn a number of cultural things as they read. The following are details to be on the lookout for: Spanish pueblo-style architecture; Indian arts and crafts; Spanish food; Indian food; Indian pueblo life; Indian social practices (manners); Indian spiritual beliefs.

History Activities for *The Discovery*

Third/Fourth: Playing the way kids did on the home front during World War II will help you to "experience" history. Spend one day or a recess playing only the kinds of games Will and Fawn had available to them, such as riding bikes and climbing trees. See what entertainments you can find in the book. Remember, no TV or computer games allowed; don't use anything that couldn't have been found "back then." Fawn and Will could pretty much run all over town by themselves, and you probably aren't allowed to do that, so you'll have to adapt the activities to your mom and dad's limits. Once you've had your Forties Play Day, report to the class or teacher what it was like being a Home-Front Kid for a day.

Fifth/Sixth: Ask your parents to help you figure out who is the oldest ancestor on your family tree that anybody knows anything about. Gather whatever information you can about him or her, and think about how that person's life has affected yours. Even if that ancestor is no longer living, write a letter to him or her, either thanking him or giving him what for!

Seventh/Eighth: Find out more about the censoring of letters that went back and forth overseas between soldiers and their loved ones. Some books in your libraries will have samples, and some of your older relatives may have even saved some. Write a letter to someone fighting overseas. Then write the reply, and highlight the things the censors might have blacked out if it had been a real letter.

The Mirage

Europe was the focus of war attention in the early summer of 1944, as word filtered out that the Allied forces were planning a huge offensive against the Nazis. On June 6, 1944—a date that became known as D-Day—156,000 American, British, and Canadian troops went ashore on the beaches of Normandy, France, leading the way for two million more men who would turn the tide of the war in the European theater.

It took two divisions an entire day to fight their way off of Omaha Beach under German fire and onto the bluff, leaving another 2,500 casualties. Allied casualties the first day totaled ten thousand.

By the second day, the rough beginning smoothed out somewhat as the land battle began. The Germans were unable to push the Allies back—though it still took until August 25th to achieve significant victories. The Allied air and artillery power, including their warships at sea, were too much for the Germans. Paris was liberated and most of France recaptured. The Germans were in full retreat, and for the first time the end of the war in Europe was clearly in sight.

Hitler was not silent during the fray. On June 13, 1944, he ordered jet-propelled rockets to be fired on London. The onslaught caused widespread damage and killed thousands of people. The Germans fired on Paris on September 6, and then again on London, killing another 2,500 people. Frightening rumors began to circulate that the Germans were developing "wonder weapons" that would win the war for them.

But the Allies fought on, racing across France after D-Day. Toward the end of June, 1944, Soviet forces smashed through the German Army Group Centre, in what has become known as the Big Blitzkrieg, and all but destroyed it.

Meanwhile, in the conflict with the Japanese, on June 15, 1944, Allied Marines landed on Saipan in the Marianas because it had a highly usable harbor. Our naval forces defeated the Japanese Navy in the Battle of the Philippine Sea on June 21, 1944, with the use of submarines covering American landing operations and allowing for the interception of Japanese fighter planes. The Japanese withdrew and were unable to bring in reinforcements to the Marianas. In three weeks of tough fighting, the Japanese tried suicidal attacks with bayonets, but they were eventually repulsed. On July 9, 1944, American Marines hoisted the U.S. flag and then moved on to Tinian, the next island in the Marianas, with a surprise backdoor landing while the Japanese waited for an assault on the main beach. Now that the Allies held the Mariana Islands and had bases there, they were able to attack Guam, using long-range bombers and huge B-29s to win the island back.

Home-Front Details in *The Mirage*

With the Allies racing across France after D-Day and closing the net around Japan in the Pacific, industry in the States was operating at full blast. As a result of the victories, shortages began to ease and the OPA (Office of Price Administration) lifted the rationing on canned foods and some meats. But almost as soon as the controls were eased, the shortages returned, and in August 1944, rationing of pork loin, ham, and canned fish resumed.

Other home-front details in Book 2 include: blackouts; air raid wardens; the filtering in of rumors about concentration camps where Jews were being kept in Europe; the effect of the war on baseball; special prayer services for the war; Red Cross volunteer work; zoot suits; revival of patriotism after D-Day; recycling for the war; donating blood; newspaper casualty lists; war songs; radio news.

History Activities for *The Mirage*

Third/Fourth: Even as I am writing this teaching guide for you, America is at war again. What kinds of things did Will and Fawn do to help with the war effort? What things can you do right now to help with America's War on Terrorism? Make a list of possibilities and choose one of them to do. Share what you've done with your teacher or class.

Fifth/Sixth: You learn from *The Mirage* about the Opportunity School, a special educational program (that actually existed in Santa Fe) for kids with mental handicaps. Learn about such a school in your area, maybe even going there for a visit. Make a chart comparing the two schools.

Seventh/Eighth: Find out more about the first hints from Europe that the persecution of Jews was being carried out in cruel ways. Write an exposé like Will and Fawn would have done in their newspaper, using the first dribbled-out facts.

The Stand

As our story in Book 3 opens in the fall of 1944, rumor has it that the war in Europe will be over by Christmas. There was reason for optimism. General Eisenhower, commander of the Allied land forces in Europe, had several U.S. Army groups driving flat-out across France toward the German border, and the Germans were in full retreat before them. Total defeat of the Germans seemed inevitable as the British Army liberated Brussels on September 4 and Antwerp on September 5. It only had another 65 miles to go to enter Germany and end the war.

On the Pacific front, October 1944 brought news of the invasion of the Philippines by the Allies. Victory came at a price as several U.S. ships were lost when the Japanese started using kamikaze bombers—Japanese pilots willing to lose their lives in order to hit their targets. Eventually, the Allies emerged victorious.

Will, like actual kids living on the home front in 1944, became familiar with terms the generation before them had never heard of: PT boats, fighter pilots, parachuting behind enemy lines, tail gunners, flying fortresses, the P-51 Mustang fighter plane, and the new military vehicle called the Jeep.

Home-Front Details in *The Stand*

GI Bill of Rights passed by Congress; school vaccinations; soda shops; discrimination against Japanese-Americans; relocation camps; the handling of the subject of war in the classroom; Tojos; scarcity of cars; newsreels.

History Activities for *The Stand*

Third/Fourth: Most kids Fawn and Will's age didn't get to become friends with Japanese-American children who had been forced to live in relocation camps. Imagine that it's 1944 and you *have* had that chance, as our characters did. Make a picture book for your other friends, showing what it's like to be a Japanese youngster like Ken and Emi during World War II, living in a relocation camp. Your pictures can be your own drawings or photocopies of pictures from books, and each one should have a short paragraph or statement explaining some part of their life in the camp.

Fifth/Sixth: Imagine that you are part of a delegation going to President Roosevelt to ask that the Japanese-Americans be released from their camps and be allowed to return to their own homes. Knowing all that Fawn and Will know, put together the speech that you would give President Roosevelt. You may want to write it out first; at least outline it, gathering information from the book. Then put your speech on tape if you can or simply deliver it to your class or teacher, giving it all the passion you can muster!

Seventh/Eighth: Look into the background for the relocation of Japanese-Americans right at the beginning of the war. Then make a timeline from the attack on Pearl Harbor to the time when the relocation order was reversed, showing the most important events. Make your timeline as clear and as creative as possible, as if you were going to use it to show Will, Fawn, and Abe exactly how it all happened.

The Mission

Book 4 opens in the winter of 1944, just before Christmas. Despite earlier predictions, it doesn't look as if the war in Europe is going to be over before December 25. On December 16, Hitler began his last, desperate counterattack against advancing Allied forces in Germany, which became known as the dreadful Battle of the Bulge. He started with a full-scale attack on Allied armies headed for Antwerp, but after two days of fighting had not made much progress. The Allies recovered from the initial surprise, and 35 Allied divisions banded together against what was left of the German army. By December 30, 1944, it was really over for Germany, but Hitler would not give up, and the Allies were forced to slowly push the Germans back, through snow and sub-zero temperatures. Finally, on January 28, 1945, the Battle of the Bulge officially ended, with the Allies as the victors.

The Germans had nothing to stop the Soviets on the Eastern front, either. By December 1944, Soviet troops were pushing the Germans steadily back, with German cities being destroyed around the clock by bombing. Starting January 12, 1945, the Soviets were heading for Berlin.

In the Pacific theater, on November 17, 1944, one of the American B-29s crashed into the ocean on its return flight to the Marianas. A week later, two more crashed the same way, making it clear that the U.S. needed to control the island of Iwo Jima ("sulphur island") to use for crippled bombers as an emergency landing spot. So starting in late November, U.S. planes bombed Iwo Jima for 74 consecutive days, but aerial photos showed that Japanese defenses were stronger than they'd been before the bombing started. In February 1945, a large force of Marines sailed for Iwo Jima where, unbeknownst to them, 22,000 Japanese soldiers had dug holes, tunnels, and caves and filled them with machine gun nests. The Japanese allowed the U.S. soldiers to land; when the beach was crowded with soldiers, unseen Japanese opened fire. There was nowhere to run and few places to hide. The Marines managed to fight their way off the beach and then set their sights on Mt. Suribachi, an extinct volcano on the southern tip of the island which was 550 feet high and ringed with caves and tunnels. By the end of the first week, a group of U.S. Marines reached the top and planted the U.S. flag, although the island wasn't secured until March 16, which we will discuss under *The Struggle* (Book 5).

On December 18, 1944, 1,300 of the prisoners of war taken by the Japanese at Bataan were stuffed into the hold of a former cruise liner to be taken to Japan. There was little food, air, or water on board, so some died en route. American planes attacked the ship, unaware that there were Americans on board, so the men were transferred by the Japanese to a freighter and issued one mess kit with only enough rice and water in it for six men. The prisoners resorted to licking condensation from the hull of the ship. By the time the freighter reached Kyushu Island, where it was intercepted by an American ship, only 350 prisoners were still alive to be rescued—but that was still 350 American soldiers set free.

Home-Front Details in *The Mission*

Food rationing was fully imposed again in December 1944 when the Allied advance in Europe was slowed down by the Battle of the Bulge. A fuel shortage on the home front made for a cold winter. Other home-front details in Book 4 include: comedy movies with war themes; Stars Over America Cavalcade money-raising tours; individual and group attempts to raise money for the war effort; Christmas without the loved ones who were fighting abroad; radio.

History Activities for *The Mission*

Third/Fourth: From what you've read in *The Mission*, you know that it sure wasn't easy growing up while your dad was overseas, either fighting in a war or being kept in a prison camp. Imagine that you are such a kid. Make a one-week diary out of construction paper and binder paper. Write a diary entry for each of the seven days in your week. You can draw pictures to illustrate if you want.

Fifth/Sixth: It must have been very frustrating for kids on the home front who felt they couldn't do anything to help with the war, so when the Stars Over America Cavalcade show came to town, they were probably inspired to at least raise a little money for war bonds. Find out as much as you can about the way ordinary people, even kids, did raise money for bonds, then put together an information booklet, 1940s style, entitled "How You Can Help." Illustrate if you want. Be as specific as you can.

Seventh/Eighth: Find out more about the way prisoners of war were treated by the Japanese or the Germans. Imagine that you had to tell the family of someone in one of those prison camps about the conditions there. Decide how you would do it and prepare your presentation. Would it be a frank discussion? A well-worded letter? Would you put it in the form of a prayer? Be as real as you can.

The Struggle

As Book 5 opens, it is the spring of 1945, and things are coming to a head in both theaters of the war. But Americans were continually being reminded that in order for the war to be completely over, the Axis powers—now Germany and Japan—had to surrender unconditionally. That meant that the Allies would not end the war through negotiation. The future of Germany and Japan had to be turned over to the Allies completely, or the war would go on.

In the European theater, the Allies were finally into Germany, and there they saw the truth which many had tried to deny: Six million Jews had been imprisoned, tortured, and murdered in Nazi concentration camps. The reports described unspeakable horrors. Fortunately, some of the prisoners were still alive.

Finally, Adolf Hitler saw that he had reached the point of no return, and he committed suicide in April of 1945. Shortly thereafter, on May 7, 1945, Germany surrendered unconditionally to the Allies on what became known as V-E Day—Victory in Europe. In Santa Fe, as in other cities across America, celebrations were held with citizens waving flags, ringing bells, shouting their triumph with abandon. At least one part of the long, bloody war was over, and once again there was a revival of patriotism as all eyes turned to the Pacific.

The battle on Iwo Jima, which began on February 19, 1945, and which was imprinted in the minds of Americans by the famous photograph of the Marines mounting the American flag on Mt. Suribachi, was finally won on March 16, 1945, nearly a month after the initial assault. Scattered fighting continued for a few more weeks, with the final casualty totals coming in at 6,800 Allied soldiers dead and twenty thousand others wounded. Nearly all the Japanese soldiers had died.

There was now one more island the Allies had to take before fully attacking Japan itself, and that was the island of Okinawa. On April 1, 1945, Easter Day, the attack began. Kamikaze activity, which if you'll recall involved Japanese pilots willing to sacrifice themselves in suicide missions to be certain their bombs hit their targets, went on daily. On April 6 and 7, 1945, there were 355 kamikazes in the air at once, sinking four American ships and damaging 25 more. But the suicide missions did not prevent a Japanese defeat at Okinawa on June 21, which we will discuss more fully under Book 6, *The Choice*.

Home-Front Details in *The Struggle*

Eisenhower's Waste Paper Campaign to conserve paper and other resources; people tired of war; sales taxes; dimouts; midnight curfews; government takeover of private land for war purposes; revival of cattle rustling as a result of meat shortages and rationing; magazines; stunts to make the war more endurable; conscientious objectors; school activities designed to encourage patriotism; popular movies; the death of President Roosevelt.

History Activities for *The Struggle*

Third/Fourth: Remember the diorama—three-dimensional model—Will and Miguel had to make for the Treasures of New Mexico school project? Why don't you make one that shows some form of American patriotism in the 1940s. After all, the support of the folks back home kept the soldiers going overseas.

Fifth/Sixth: Learn more about the revival of activities like cattle rustling and other illegal ways that people tried to get the things they wanted and couldn't have due to shortages and rationing. Make some posters reminding people that those activities are against the law, making the posters as if you were living during the war.

Seventh/Eighth: Learn more about conscientious objectors during World War II—why they objected to the war, and how they were treated on the home front. Then write an editorial to the newspaper, either supporting them, criticizing them, or remarking on their treatment no matter what your own opinion is. Write, of course, as if the war is currently going on.

The Choice

As Book 6 opens, the war in Europe is over and soldiers are beginning to return home, many of them blinded, missing limbs, paralyzed, and battle-scarred. All are exhausted, but they are determined to live lives that represent those who didn't make it.

One of our characters, Fawn's father, John Daniel McHorse (Dan), represents fictionally the actual Navajo Code Talkers who played an essential part in the war. During the 1930s, German anthropology students had visited the United States and gone to almost every Indian group with the intent of learning its language, should the U.S. military someday attempt to use it as a code. The only Indian group it was unable to penetrate was the isolated Navajo. In fact, at that time, only 30 people outside the Navajo tribe knew its difficult language. It was never written down and it rarely borrowed words but always invented new ones. After the U.S. entered the war, the military desperately needed to develop a code that the Axis powers could not break. In April 1942, U.S. Marine recruiters were dispatched to Navajo reservations to find its first candidates for what were to become the Navajo Code Talkers. Those chosen were sent to San Diego where the code was set. It was never broken by either the Germans or the Japanese and saved an inestimable number of lives in the course of the war. Because of their culture and previous lifestyle, the Navajos were well suited to harsh conditions and meager supplies and proved themselves adaptable to almost any situation. Unfortunately their courage and their impact on the war were not recognized publicly until 1969.

While the U.S., Great Britain, and Russia planned a conference at Potsdam, near Berlin, to decide the fate of Germany, there was still the war in the Pacific which had to come to an end. Optimism at home was high, encouraged by the sight of the picture snapped of the American flag being raised on Mt. Suribachi on posters and 3-cent postage stamps. Truly, Japan was near defeat by the summer of 1945. Her once mighty navy lay at the bottom of the Pacific Ocean. American B-29 bombers were pounding Japan's cities, causing terrible damage, but so far hadn't brought surrender. A full invasion of the Japanese mainland seemed necessary. Officials estimated that such an invasion would kill over one million more Americans and Japanese. When, Americans wondered, would the killing stop?

Unbeknownst to American citizens, an atomic bomb was being developed at Los Alamos, New Mexico, which had the potential to end the war. It was secretly tested on July 16, the very day that the Potsdam Conference began. The test was successful.

But the bomb was not used immediately. At the end of July 1945, the Allies published an ultimatum, demanding unconditional surrender of the armed forces of Japan. The demand was rejected. Leaflets were then dropped on 11 Japanese cities, warning its citizens that they were in danger of intensive aerial bombardment, but there was still no surrender. Non-atomic bombs were dropped on six of those cities on July 29, 1945. Twelve more cities were warned July 31, 1945, and four of them were bombed August 1. The final warning was issued on August 5, 1945. When the Japanese still refused to surrender, an atomic bomb was dropped on Hiroshima, Japan, the next day, destroying the entire city. On August 9, 1945, another was dropped on Nagasaki, Japan, likewise annihilating it completely.

Finally, on August 14, 1945, in a ceremony aboard the battleship USS *Missouri* in Tokyo Bay, Japanese officials signed a formal surrender ending World War II. The next day, unable to bear the shame of surrender, Japanese Vice-Admiral Ohnishi and several of his men performed hara-kiri, a ritual suicide.

And so the long war was over. The prediction made by Britain's

Prime Minister Winston Churchill had come true: there had been many disasters, immeasurable cost, and tribulation, but in the end, there had been victory.

There was, of course, great celebration throughout the Allied countries on V-J Day—Victory over Japan—but for families like Will's, the horrific waiting was not yet over. In the Pacific, GIs discovered the barbarity of the Japanese soldiers when they freed the starving Allied prisoners of war. Though all with loved ones unaccounted for hoped theirs were among them, it was a slim hope indeed, for 45 percent of the 200th and 515th Coast Artillery Regiments had lost their lives. In *The Choice*, Rudy Hutchinson is brought home alone. In actuality, the liberated prisoners of Bataan from those regiments arrived together at the train station in Lamy, New Mexico, on October 21, 1945, after three and a half years in the Japanese camps. Among the returnees was Brigadier General Charles G. Sage, commanding officer of the units. He, too, had survived the rigors, giving unselfish devotion and attention to the sick and hungry prisoners whom he considered "his boys." Several hundred relatives were on hand to greet the men at Lamy, some of them not knowing if their loved one was still alive or not. For all of them, it was also the climax to the emotional strain of more than four years of waiting.

Like many state governors, the governor of New Mexico insisted that there not be a long period of unemployment for the soldiers when they returned and were once more able to work—as had been the experience following the First World War. The state government had a fund to finance projects to provide jobs.

Emotional support was already in place. All who survived the Japanese prison camps claimed to be closer to one another than brothers. Long days of suffering, starving, and seeing their buddies die bound them together, as one put it, "with bonds of steel."

Home-Front Details in *The Choice*

Continuing shortages and rationing; adjustments to dads coming home after long absences; conjecture about what was happening up at Los

Alamos; "shell shock"; army hospitals for soldiers returning to the States; spy activity; the effects of the war on Indian pueblo life; revelation of the atomic bomb; prayer vigils for the war; V-J Day celebrations; dealing with physical and emotional changes in the returning GIs.

History Activities for *The Choice*

Third/Fourth: Plan a V-J Day celebration and invite your friends!

Fifth/Sixth: There were other places besides Los Alamos involved in the Manhattan Project, the name for the development of the atomic bomb. Find out about those. Then make a timeline that shows the steps in the process. You'll be surprised to find out how few people involved really knew what it was all about. Knowing what you know now, write on the back of your timeline whether you would have liked to have been involved in some phase of it—or not.

Seventh/Eighth: Find out more about the two sides of the question: should the U.S. have dropped atomic bombs on Japan? Write a dialogue between two people who are on different sides of the issue. You might have your teacher or another student read it aloud with you.

Literature Folder

NOTE: The literary elements dealt with in this folder are part of the five-book teaching guide curriculum. If you would like to see what other literary elements are taught in the guides, please refer to Appendix I.

ANOTHER NOTE: As you read the sections below, you'll see that some are written as if I'm talking to you, the teacher, and others are composed as if I'm chatting with the students themselves. There is no consistent reason for that variation, other than that sometimes it seemed appropriate to address you and at others to speak directly to the kids. I trust this will be apparent to you and won't cause confusion.

The Discovery

If you ask me—and sometimes people actually do!—no matter how important the lesson is in a kids' book or how wonderfully it's written, it isn't worth reading unless it tells an absorbing story. So let's consider *plot* first, as we have done in the other four guides. Plot, of course, is *what happens in a story*, and *how it happens,* and *what makes what happens captivating*. The following are suggestions for teaching plot in *The Discovery*.

Third/Fourth: At this age, concentrate on what happens and in what order. You can do this by orally summarizing the chapters together. Play a group trivia game featuring the important events, or put the things that happen in a chapter on cards, mix them up, and have the students put them back in order. You could even use these plot exercises for all six books if you're so inclined. In the **Feel-Free-to-Photocopy Folder**, you'll find a plot sheet titled, "Discover the Mistakes" to use if you want to continue working on plot in *The Discovery*.

Fifth/Sixth: Kids at this age really get into the whole idea of cause-and-effect. It's the "If I hadn't done this, then that wouldn't have happened" thing. They're very fact-oriented and like to know the reasons for things—and can pick out an illogical flaw in a plot like little hawks! Use the Feel-Free-to-Photocopy sheet titled, "Discovering Why." Then, if you want to continue discussing cause-and-effect, talk with your student(s) about a time in their own lives when one thing definitely led to another—or use that topic as a free-writing journal entry.

Seventh/Eighth: In the other four teaching guides, we've talked about plot structure with this age group. For a review of those (or in case by some HUGE oversight you aren't familiar with the other guides!), use the Feel-Free-to-Photocopy sheet titled, "The Plot Thickens." Then turn to critiquing the plot. Ask your seventh or eighth grader(s) the following questions, encouraging them to be as persnickety as possible:

- *Do you get enough background information to start off with to keep you from getting confused or being left in the dark?*
- *Do you get too MUCH background information and wish the story would just move on?*

- *Does the plot build: like somebody hauling a boulder uphill? in fits and starts like a radio that isn't tuned to the station? as smoothly as a well-oiled machine? so fast you can't keep up with it?*
- *Was the climax exciting or satisfying enough for you?*
- *Were there any unanswered questions at the end? (except for the ones you're going to expect to be answered in the next book)*

The Mirage

Since we're really getting acquainted with Will, Fawn, Mom, and Bud by now, and we're adding new people like Abe, Mr. Spitz, and the Three Amigos, Book 2 is a good place to talk about *characters*. As you work on *characterization* with kids on any grade level, treat the people on the page as real folks that they can get to know. Hopefully they'll continue that habit in future books they read.

Third/Fourth: Let's review the whole idea of looking at characters as real people. In Book 2, Abe delights in having letters read to him that were written by his mom and dad, whom he hasn't seen since he was a little guy. Why don't you do the same thing? Choose two of the characters that you like the most in *The Mirage* and have those characters each write a letter to the other one, telling all about themselves. If you're just getting started in writing, try composing telegrams instead. Include as much about the character as you can. Doing the Feel-Free-to-Photocopy sheet entitled, "Let Me Tell You a Little About Myself" first will help you.

Fifth/Sixth: One of the most interesting things about people is the way they get along—or don't get along. It's the same in literature. Who would want to read a book about only one character—or even one about just two characters who ALWAYS got along? Choose two characters in *The Mirage* who don't have too many conflicts with each other and are able to work out the ones they DO have. Then choose two who couldn't get along if you paid them to! Using those two sets of characters, complete the Feel-Free-to-Photocopy sheet entitled "Why Can't Everybody Just Get Along?" Then have your teacher give you a problem for the first set of characters to work out. Do that as a role play. Then try the other two characters, the ones that couldn't get along even in a perfect world. Pretty interesting, huh? (For you, Teacher, possible subjects might be: a rule that to one character seems stupid; whether it's important to keep up with the news; what to do about bullies; dealing with kids that are way "different"; what to do when your parent is in a bad mood.)

Seventh/Eighth: Every character in a story should have a purpose for being there. Use the Feel-Free-to-Photocopy sheet entitled, "Good Guys and Bad Guys" to learn what some of those main purposes might be and the literary terms that identify them. (You will then feel very smart!) Once you've done that, pick one character—besides Will—that you think the story couldn't live without, and talk with your teacher or class about why. You might even want to have a debate about this question: if the editor said the author had to get rid of one character, which one could it possibly be, and what other changes would have to be made in the story for it to still survive without that character?

The Stand

Because the entire Christian Heritage Series is historical fiction, this might be a good time to introduce the concept of that *genre*. You might start by gathering some books of different genres, spreading them out, and helping your student(s) identify them. Depending on your age group, choices might include mystery, science fiction, fantasy, romance, adventure, historical fiction, and legal or political thriller. Then explain that you'll be focusing on historical fiction—what makes for good books in that genre and how it's different from the other types of fiction.

Third/Fourth: At this level, you might want to keep your focus simply on the difference between fact and fiction in *The Stand*. The Feel-Free-to-Photocopy sheet titled, "Come On—What *Really* Happened?" will be helpful. Then read aloud some nonfiction about Japanese relocation camps and ask student(s) to talk about the differences between that and *The Stand*. The book *I Am an American* by Jerry Stanley (Crown Publishers, 1994) is an excellent choice.

Fifth/Sixth: Kids of this age can understand how fact and fiction can be mixed together, which can then be a fun way for them to show what they're learning in their other historical studies. Start with the Feel-Free-to-Photocopy sheet entitled "Mixing It Up—Without Getting Mixed Up!" Then have student(s) find another instance in the book not used on the sheet in which fact and fiction are woven together. With a group you can have a contest to see who can find the most. (Tootsie Rolls or Juicy Fruit gum might make a good prize, since Will and Fawn enjoy them so much—and maybe just this one time wouldn't be SO bad for the teeth!)

Seventh/Eighth: As natural critics of just about everything, seventh- and eighth-graders enjoy checking things out to make sure the author knows her stuff. Use the same photocopy sheet the fifth- and sixth-graders used ("Mixing It Up—Without Getting Mixed Up!") to find areas where historical facts are introduced into the story. Then send student(s) on a mission to look up those facts to check out their accuracy. (And if you find a mistake—let me know!)

The Mission

I think it's important to talk about *theme* often when you're enjoying literature—not in terms of some search for minuscule details of hidden meaning (didn't you hate that in school?), but for a totally fulfilling experience in reading a book. If you don't take something away from it with you, what's the point? As I've said before, it's important for any reader to feel that a book has "done something" for him or her—reached out with something about life he or she had never thought about before, or thought about but wondered if anybody else did. A study of theme is simply to help your student(s) decide what a book has to say and whether that relates to them in any meaningful way.

Third/Fourth: A good way to approach theme is to ask, "How did Will change from the beginning of the book to the end of the book? What did he learn?" That's the theme. See if you can all agree on one statement—or maybe two. The Feel-Free-to-Photocopy sheet entitled, "Boy, Has *He* Changed!" will help.

Fifth/Sixth: If a book doesn't say something that relates to you and your life, it's not going to mean much to you. Most of the "fan mail" I get comments that something in the book "was just like me!" With that in mind, start with the Feel-Free-to-Photocopy sheet entitled "Get a Clue, Will!" Then discuss with your teacher or your class—or even in your private journal—times in your life when you've made mistakes similar to the ones Will made in *The Mission*. Talk candidly about how it turned out—and how it might have turned out differently if you'd approached things the way Will did in the end.

Seventh/Eighth: You're at a point in your life where you can start to consider this question about any book you read: was the theme worth learning? Use the Feel-Free-to-Photocopy sheet entitled "Get a Clue, Will!" to determine what the theme of *The Mission* is. Then ask yourself these questions and either discuss your answers with your teacher or class, or write your answers in your private journal.

- *Do I already know all that stuff about life?*
- *Does it make any difference in anything I'm dealing with in my life right now?*
- *COULD it make a difference?*
- *Do I know anybody else it could help?*

- *Do I even believe it's true?*
- *Do I need to explore this further?*
- *Do I need to pray about it?*

The Struggle

Books 1 through 4 of The Santa Fe Years have primarily taken place in town or on the San Ildefonso Pueblo. In Book 5 we move south of town, into the New Mexico high desert terrain, so this is a good place to talk about *setting*. While setting is both the place and the time of a book, we discuss the historical time in so many other sections of the guide, we'll focus on place here. Hopefully you and your students will enjoy this little journey into one of the most beautiful places in the world.

Third/Fourth: The way Olive lives is VERY different from the way Will and Fawn live. Use the Feel-Free-to-Photocopy sheet entitled "Two Different Worlds" to get started on that concept. Have your students draw pictures, one of Will's house and one of Olive's, using details from the book. Then talk with your student(s) about which environment they would prefer.

Fifth/Sixth: We know how different the town of Santa Fe is from the environment Olive lives in, and it is the language-that-creates-pictures that helps us as readers to see that. First use the Feel-Free-to-Photocopy sheet entitled "I Can Just *See* It!" Then, using the lists of words you've gathered while completing the sheet, create two images of the two places using only the lists. Your images don't have to be realistic pictures, although they CAN be. They can also be combinations of colors and shapes, or they can simply be a symbol of each place. Create whatever you want, based on the language you've just studied.

Seventh/Eighth: It's time to consider the purpose of setting. Sure, you have to have a time and a place for things to happen or it would be pretty weird, but does that setting contribute to the character, the plot, and the theme? Would it make any difference if it were set anywhere else at any other time? Do the Feel-Free-to-Photocopy sheet entitled "What Difference Does It Make?" Then do a little research on what was happening on the home front in some other place in America during World War II. What about New York City? How about California? Consider using the place where one of your grandparents lived as a kid during the war so you can do a personal interview. Discuss with your teacher or class how our story would have been different if its setting had been in that place instead.

The Choice

The *impact* that a book has is somewhat like its theme, but it's a little more abstract. I'm convinced, however, that even the youngest reader can understand the concept and increase his or her enjoyment of future books as a result. Since this is such an individual real-life thing, there are no Feel-Free-to-Photocopy sheets for this section on any of the grade levels, so that nothing about it feels like a "school assignment."

Third/Fourth: Now that you've read all six of the books in The Santa Fe Years, there are some things you know now that maybe you didn't know before, personal things that you could only know by either experiencing them yourself or reading about someone else's experience. For example, *what do you now know about being separated from someone you love for a very long time?* Think about what it would be like if your mom or dad or someone else very close to you had to be away from you for three or four years, the way Will's dad was. Think about how you might feel. What difference would it make in the way you lived every day? What things would you miss the most? How would you yourself have to change? After you've thought about it and maybe talked about it with your teacher or class, write a letter to that person, telling him or her all those things. Chances are, you'll want to deliver that letter as a gift. You couldn't give a better one.

Fifth/Sixth: Even as I'm writing this guide, the United States is involved in a war that may go on for a long time, though hopefully not as long as World War II. If you haven't been affected by the War on Terrorism, you probably will be in some way as the fighting continues. Having read The Santa Fe Years books, hopefully you know what war can be like for the people who are here at home while the battles rage on the other side of the ocean. From what you've learned, write a letter or make a list on a poster that would help other kids prepare for what might be ahead. Think very carefully about the sacrifices Will and his friends and family had to make—not just the physical ones, like only being able to buy so much gas, but the emotional ones as well, like having to grow up fast and missing important people in their lives. You may actually be able to help someone with what you've learned.

Seventh/Eighth: One of the things that was produced during World War II which has continued to be a threat to us ever since is the atomic bomb. We learn some things about it in Book 6 of The Santa Fe Years—not only the historical facts, but how it affected individual people's lives, even if it was merely in their thoughts. The United States is at war again as I write this guide, and there is some fear that the terrorists we are fighting have access to atomic weapons. Use all that you've learned in *The Choice*, as well as other information you look up for yourself if you want to, to write an open letter to all kids your age, sharing your knowledge and helping them prepare themselves for the feelings that may arise if an atomic bomb is used at some time in our present war. Don't think of it as a fear letter. Think of it as a way to help other kids understand, the way you now do. After all, that's the whole purpose of education.

Writing Folder

NOTE: The writing elements dealt with in this folder are part of the five-book teaching guide curriculum. If you would like to see what other elements are taught in which guides, please refer to Appendix II.

ANOTHER NOTE: Because of the nature of this approach to fiction, it might be best to do the writing strand after ALL six books have been read.

The writing strand for The Santa Fe Years focuses on writing fiction for fun, and the writing activities for each book involve a particular aspect of fiction purely on an enjoyment level. Not everyone can be a publishable fiction writer, but I believe everyone can derive some delight from dabbling in it—and who knows whether you'll discover a budding author in the process!

Before you begin, please read this important message: Grammar, punctuation, mechanics, usage—those things are definitely important, but deal with them LAST! Before you worry about those finishing details, your students need to learn to gather information, organize it, structure the piece, write, revise, rearrange, and rewrite. After all of that, THEN they can be concerned with what's spelled wrong, where the commas should go, and so on. Otherwise, they will be trying to hang up wallpaper before the drywall goes on. Can you tell I feel strongly about this? Nothing squelches good writing more than too much attention to grammatical detail too soon.

Also, if your students' usage and mechanics are deficient, concentrate on one skill at a time. Look for the weakest one and get that pretty well straightened out before you move on. If you point out all the mistakes at once, the student is likely to be overwhelmed and simply give up. Not every paper has to be grammatically perfect as long as progress is being made.

The Discovery

Writing Fiction for Fun/ Where Do Ideas Come From?

After completing the Feel-Free-to-Photocopy sheet, you might want to do one of the following:

Third/Fourth:

- Find three ideas for stories in your social studies book/curriculum.
- Find two ideas for stories in your favorite nonfiction book (you know, that great book on dinosaurs or horses or airplanes or dollhouses that you look at over and over).
- Find one idea for a story by asking an adult what it was like when he or she was a kid your age.

Fifth/Sixth:

- Find three ideas for stories in your science book/curriculum.
- Find two ideas for stories by looking through a newspaper.

- Find one idea for a story by interviewing someone whose life has been very different from yours.

Seventh/Eighth:

- Find one idea for a story by flipping through your math book/curriculum.
- Find three ideas for stories from the nonfiction articles in a magazine.
- Find two ideas for stories by watching strangers in a public place.

The Mirage

Writing Fiction for Fun/ Creating Characters

After completing the Feel-Free-to-Photocopy sheet, do ALL of the following:

Third/Fourth: Using ONE of the ideas you came up with in your activities for *The Discovery*:

- Think of a name, age, and gender (that means boy or girl) for a main character.
- Give that character a problem—something he or she wants very badly, something he or she wants to change, or something he or she is really afraid will happen.
- Think of another character who makes that problem even worse for your main character—stands in the way of your main character getting what he or she wants, won't allow the change your main character wants, or makes your main character even more afraid. Give this "problem character" a name, age, and gender.

Fifth/Sixth: Using ONE of the ideas you came up with in your activities for *The Discovery*:

- Think of a name, age, and gender for a main character. Give that character two physical traits and two personality traits.
- Give that character a problem—a desire that hasn't been fulfilled, a needed change that hasn't happened, a fear that hasn't been overcome, or a goal that hasn't been reached.
- Think of another character who makes the problem even worse for your main character. Give this problem character name, age, gender, two physical traits, and two personality traits.

Seventh/Eighth: Using ONE of the ideas you came up with in your activities for *The Discovery*:

- Think of a name, age, and gender for a protagonist. Give that character two physical traits and two personality traits. Then give that character a problem—maybe a goal or desire that hasn't been fulfilled yet, or a hang-up that constantly gets in his or her way (like shyness or body image or feeling different from everybody else).
- Give that protagonist a friend—a secondary character who tries to help. Give THAT character one physical trait and one personality trait. Decide what his or her relationship is to the protagonist (sister, brother, same-age friend, adult friend, parent, school janitor—use your imagination!).
- Think of a name, age, and gender for an antagonist—the character who constantly makes the protagonist's problem worse. Then give THAT character two physical traits, two personality traits, and one hang-up that your protagonist might be able to take advantage of at some point. (Example: really likes to be flattered, will do anything for a hot Krispy Kreme donut—that kind of thing.)

The Stand

Writing Fiction for Fun/ Imagining Setting

After completing the Feel-Free-to-Photocopy sheet, do ALL of the following:

Third/Fourth: Continuing with your same story idea—

- Choose a place for your story. Will it be in a big city? A school? A baseball diamond? A ballet studio?
- Choose a time for your story. Is it happening in the present time, as it would today? Do you have a historical period in mind, like the pioneer days or the 1970s?
- Choose a season for your story—spring, summer, winter, or fall.

Fifth/Sixth: Continuing with your same story idea—

- Choose a specific place for your story. Don't say simply "in New York City" but "in Manhattan" or "in Brooklyn." If you want your place to be even more specific, don't say simply "in a school" but "in a middle school."
- Choose a specific time period for your story. That means year and season. Some examples would be "the summer of 1951," "December 1777," "the fall of 2002."
- Choose two detailed time/places for two different scenes in your story. For instance, in a story set in "the summer of 1951 in Brooklyn," one scene could take place at night on the front porch and the other could happen the next morning at the police station. This might change later as you build your plot, but it may also give you ideas FOR your plot.

Seventh/Eighth: Continuing with your same story idea—

- Choose a specific place for your story, such as the slums of Cleveland, Ohio, a tall skyscraper in San Francisco, or a tomb in one of the pyramids of Egypt.
- Select a specific time for your story, such as the dead of winter in 1932, April in today's time, or the year 400 B.C. in the middle of summer.
- Picture the details of a VERY specific setting. For example, if your story takes place in the slums of Cleveland, Ohio, in the dead of winter in 1932, describe the dreary basement apartment where your protagonist lives, right down to the rats in the corners and the naked lightbulb hanging from the ceiling.

The Mission

Writing Fiction for Fun/ Building Plot

After completing the Feel-Free-to Photocopy sheet, do ALL of the following for your grade level.

Third/Fourth: Continuing with your same story idea—

- Remember that problem you gave your main character up in the character section? Think of one way that problem could get worse. For example, let's say your character's problem is that he is afraid of the water, and you set your story on the beach in summer. Then you could make his problem worse by having a girl show up, and because she's his problem character who is always making fun of him for being a "scaredy-cat," he desperately wants to impress her.
- Now make that problem even worse. In our example, your main character gets in the water to show the girl that he isn't a chicken, and his bathing suit comes off.

- Now make that problem worse still. Still using our example, perhaps here comes a shark. Now your main character has a real dilemma! If he comes out of the water to escape the shark, he's going to be buck naked!

- Finally, decide how your character is going to solve that problem. In our naked-swimmer-shark-girl-on-the-beach story, perhaps he can shout that there's a dune buggy headed right for her from behind, and then he can run like the dickens for his towel when she turns around to look.

Fifth/Sixth: Continuing with your same story idea—

- Remember that problem you created for your main character up in the character section? Placing the scene in one of the two scene-settings you described in the setting section, let the problem character make that problem even worse for your main character. For instance, it's the summer of 1951 on a front porch of a house in Brooklyn. Your main character has had to move there from someplace else so she's in a strange neighborhood and none of the kids on the street will accept her, especially her problem character, the local bully girl. In this first scene, which takes place in the evening, your main character may witness the bully girl stealing somebody else's bicycle. Now she REALLY has a problem. If she tells the bicycle owner who took it, she might make a friend—but she will also certainly turn Bully Girl into her WORST enemy.

- In your second setting scene, make the problem even *worse*. Using our example, perhaps the next morning as your main character sets out to tell the bicycle owner who took her bike, she sees the destroyed bike lying in the middle of her own front yard—and here comes the owner, accompanied by the bully girl, who has told her that your main character took the bike and messed it up. It becomes clear to you at this point that you don't want your second scene to take place at the police station—it's going to have to happen in the front yard, and that's okay. It's all right to change your plan. After all, you're the author!

- Now decide how your main character is going to solve her problem. In our example, she could use one of those personality traits you gave her—maybe her talent for being an actress—and throw herself over the bike, crying and wailing to the bike's owner that she knows exactly how she must feel to see her prized bicycle in such a state, going on with hysteria until the bully gets disgusted and walks away. THEN your main character could tell the bike's owner the real story and they could decide to team up with all the other bullied kids on the street to render the Bully Girl powerless over them. See how that works?

Seventh/Eighth: Using your same story idea, setting and characters—

- Remember that protagonist you created and the problem you gave him/her? Putting that character in your specific setting, allow your antagonist to make the protagonist's problem even worse. For example, if your protagonist has just lost his job as a circus clown in Cleveland in 1932 and has no money, the antagonist, who is the landlord, could show up in that dreary basement apartment and tell our clown that he has 10 days to come up with the rent or he's on the street.
- Remember the friend you created for your protagonist? Let the friend try to help, only to make matters far worse. In our example, if the friend is a beautiful trapeze artist, they could plan for her to swing in through the window of the landlord's house and try to sweet-talk him into giving our protagonist more time. But the protagonist, who is a clown, not a rigger, gets the ropes all fouled up and our trapeze artist winds up falling through the roof, making matters almost impossible—since he now owes not only rent, but repairs on the landlord's house as well.
- Remember that hang-up you gave your antagonist? Use that to help your protagonist solve the problem. Let's say the landlord, our antagonist, doesn't want his fiancée to know what a louse he is. Our clown could tell the landlord to come on over and evict him because he doesn't have the money, but our clown could also cleverly invite

the landlord's fiancée as well, unbeknownst to the evil landlord. Once she sees how cold he is being, she will not only convince him to treat our clown fairly, but will offer to hire our clown to perform at birthday parties for her endless line of nieces and nephews. Get the idea?

The Struggle

Writing Fiction for Fun/ Starting to Write Your Story

After completing the Feel-Free-to-Photocopy sheet, do ALL of the following for your grade level. It will be helpful later on for you to skip lines as you write (write only on every other line of your paper).

Third/Fourth: Using everything you have come up with for your story so far—

- Start writing your story, NOT worrying about spelling or punctuation or anything else except telling the story. Don't even worry about how it sounds—just write. Start right where the main character is in the middle of his or her problem. Using our beach example, begin with your main character just stretching out on his blanket and wishing he weren't so afraid of the water—and here comes that nasty girl who is always giving him a hard time. She says something evil to him like, "Hey, scaredy-cat. How come you're not in the water?"
- Now write the next part, where the problem gets worse. In the example, you would describe our poor main character slowly going to the water. Then you'd write about his suddenly realizing that his bathing suit is slipping down past his ankles and disappearing into the ocean. He glances at the beach where Nasty Girl is watching his every move and tries not to let her know that he is now entirely naked under the water.

- Go on to write about the problem getting even *worse*, just as you planned it. In our example, you would describe our main character spotting the shark's fin just yards from him and his heart stopping as he gasps for air and swims frantically toward the shore—only to remember that if he gets out of the water to save himself, he's never going to hear the end of it from Nasty Girl that he is now suitless.

- And finally, write about the triumphant solution. Continuing with our example, the main character shouts to the girl that a dune buggy is about to hit her from behind. He gives such a convincing performance that she whirls around, giving him time to haul himself out of the water, mere inches from the shark's teeth, and wrap himself in a towel. By the time Nasty Girl turns around to yell at him for lying to her, he is safely covered up and can even say, "Fooled you, didn't I?"

Fifth/Sixth: Continuing with all that you've planned above for your story, simply tell the story. Do NOT worry about grammar, spelling, or even how the thing sounds. Just write down the tale, just as you've seen it in your mind. Here's a process to use:

- Start with your main character smack in the middle of his or her problem. Don't worry about giving a bunch of background. Just tell enough so the reader won't be confused. Using our example of the girl with the Bully Girl problem, you would start with her slumping on the porch swing at dusk, feeling so lonely she's about to cry. She sees a shadowy form pass the house, headed for the one next door. It's Bully Girl acting suspicious.

- Now write about the problem getting worse, as you've planned it, with all the feeling you can muster. In our example, you would show your main character squatting down to look through the slats of the porch railing so she wouldn't be seen. You would portray her mouth going dry as she watches Bully Girl sneak into the next door neighbor's garage and come out with a bicycle that isn't hers. As you wrote about Bully Girl riding away on it in the gathering darkness, you'd also describe the mental tennis match going on inside your main character's head. Should she tell on the bully and leave herself open to more bullying? But that might also mean that the girl whose bike was stolen might like her better. Yet is it worth the risk? You'd write about her going inside to spend a sleepless night of worry.

- Now move on to the problem getting worse, just as you've planned it. Using our example, you would write about our main character stepping out into the sunlight on the front porch the next morning and seeing the smashed bicycle on her front lawn. You'd describe her horror, just as she sees Bully Girl dragging the bike owner over to see it. You would write about the possible solutions flipping through her head. And then the idea comes to her. Writing for all you're worth, you'd describe your main character hurling herself down the steps and across the yard, throwing herself dramatically across the bicycle and breaking into false tears. Right about now you would realize that you needed to give a hint about this talent your main character has a little earlier in the story, so you'd go back to the first scene at the very beginning and describe her wishing she were back in Atlanta where she had been the star of every school play.

- At last you can write about the victory! Your main character solves the problem, just as you planned, although don't be afraid to change a detail or two or use another brilliant solution that pops into your head. In our example story, you would write about the bully girl saying, "I don't believe this! She's hysterical! Pull yourself together, girl!" and finally giving up and stomping away, muttering under her breath. Then you would describe your main character peeking to make sure Bully Girl is gone and then immediately ceasing to cry and hopping up and telling the neighbor girl the true story. You'd write about the change coming over the neighbor girl's face and the way she suddenly warms up to the main character. With relish, you would deliciously write about their putting their heads together to scheme, thus ending the story.

Seventh/Eighth: Continuing with all that you've planned above for your story, simply tell the story. Do NOT worry about grammar, spelling, or even how the thing sounds. Write down the tale, just as you've seen it in your mind. Here's a process to use:

- Start with your main character smack in the middle of his or her problem. Don't worry about giving a bunch of background. Using our example of the down-and-out clown, you might start with a sentence such as, "Freddie—formerly known as Bubbles the Clown—was taking off his makeup for the last time. It was cold in the damp basement apartment, and there wasn't much chance of its getting any warmer, since without the circus job now, there was little hope that he'd be able to pay the heating bill, much less the rent. He sighed deeply as he pulled off the big red nose that had always made the children laugh. He'd never felt less like laughing himself in his whole life."
- Using your plot plan—and your character plan—and your setting plan—continue to write, moving on to the part where your antagonist makes the problem worse for the protagonist. In our example, Bubbles hears a knock on the door, and he knows instinctively who it is. You continue writing, describing Mr. Landlord in all his coldness and nastiness. You tell in detail how he looks as he hands Bubbles the warning notice, how he talks as he explains to Bubbles that he needs the money so that he and his fiancée can finally be married. You describe Bubbles' thoughts as Mr. Landlord leaves and his knowledge that the landlord would do anything to keep his fiancée from knowing what a louse he is.
- Keep writing, following your plan. Trapeze Lady comes by and finds Bubbles in a state of despair. You describe their conversation as they huddle together in the gloomy apartment and come up with the only plan that gives them any hope. You detail Bubbles rigging the ropes from a tall tree over Mr. Landlord's house and Trapeze Lady braving the cold to attempt to swing in through the window. Make it vivid as Bubbles loses his grip on the rope and sends Trapeze Lady right through the roof. He can hear her shouting at

the landlord as he shouts back, so he knows she isn't hurt. But that's the only good thing, you write. You describe Mr. Landlord storming out of his house into the snow, shaking his fist at Bubbles, shouting that he not only has to pay the rent within 10 days, but he has to come up with the cash for the repair of the roof as well.

- Finally you can move on to describing the solution to the hopeless problem you've created for your poor protagonist. In our example, you'd write about Bubbles in the depths of his despair muttering to himself that if only the landlord's fiancée knew what a jerk he was being, she'd threaten not to marry him. Suddenly, you write, he sees a way to get the landlord to change his mind. He'll ask the landlord over and, without telling the landlord, the fiancée as well. Your fingers are flying now as you write about Bubbles dashing to answer the door of his apartment to let the landlord's fiancée in. You describe Bubbles playing up his hungry, cold, despondent state and Fiancée nearly in tears with sympathy for him. And then the victory—you describe Mr. Landlord storming in with his hand out for money and seeing his beloved staring at him with dagger eyes. You hardly know what to write next—Bubbles' feeling of anticipation, the look on Mr. Landlord's face, or the way Fiancée walks over and gives him a piece of her mind. But you write it all, anxious to get to the part where Fiancée turns warmly to Bubbles and offers to hire him. You include the rush of relief that comes over Bubbles, as well as the purple rage on Mr. Landlord's face that he is trying so hard to cover, as Fiancée tells him to lower Bubbles' rent and give him extra time to pay—or else she's breaking off the engagement. Now you go with your own story, just like that.

The Choice

Writing Fiction for Fun/ Polishing It Up

After completing the Feel-Free-to-Photocopy sheet, do ALL of the following for your grade level.

Third/Fourth: What you have written is your rough draft. That means you have the important stuff down, but you'll want to polish it up. This part is like putting the decorations on the cookies or putting the cool stickers on your model airplane. Let it be fun by following this process. And by the way, since this is a ROUGH draft, scratch things out as you need to, scrunch things between the lines, draw arrows to the margins to put stuff in. The messier the better, because it means you're really working on your story. Okay—here we go!

- First, make sure your very first sentence grabs the reader's attention. If it's something like, "Randy was sitting on the beach wishing he wasn't afraid of the water," that's okay, but does it really GRAB somebody and make him or her want to read on? What if you used, "'I hate the beach,' Randy said to himself as he flopped down on his blanket in the sand. 'I hate it almost as much as I hate Agnes Anne Porter.'" Wouldn't that be more eye-catching?
- Read through your story and make sure all the events in your plot are in order and that you haven't left anything out. In our sample story, it wouldn't work to wait until Randy is already in the water before you tell that he's afraid of it, right? That's the kind of thing you're looking for.
- Be sure the reader will know where and when the story is taking place. That ought to happen pretty early in the story. In our example story, the first sentence, "'I hate the beach,' Randy said to himself as he flopped down on his blanket in the sand," tells us that. If you haven't done that, make a change somewhere in the first

couple of sentences.

- Make sure the reader can really picture your main character and his or her problem character. Look for at least name, age, gender, and main problem, but SHOWN, not just told. In our example story, we'd want to change this:

  Randy was a nine-year-old boy who was afraid of the water.

  To this:

  Randy looked gloomily at the water and thought to himself, "I feel like a moron. How many other nine-year-old boys are afraid to go swimming?"

- Finally, read through your story and make sure it's exactly the way you want it. If you think one word might sound better than another in your head, try it. If you want to tell the color of your main character's hair, go for it. It's your story, born in your imagination, so you're the boss.

- If you really like it, now is the time to get some help with the spelling and punctuation and usage, and then produce a clean, correct-as-you-can-make-it copy. By now it's a work of art that belongs to you, so you might want to make a cover for it or even illustrate it. Send it to your grandmother or stick it on the refrigerator with a magnet or ask the whole family to listen to you read it out loud. You've done something pretty complicated, my friend. Congratulations.

Fifth/Sixth: What you've written is your rough draft. That means you have the important stuff down, but you'll want to polish it up. This part is like putting the decorations on the cookies or putting the cool stickers on your model airplane. Let it be fun by following this process. (And by the way, since this is a ROUGH draft, scratch things out as you need to, scrunch things between the lines, draw arrows to the margins to put stuff in. The messier the better, because it means you're really working on your story.) Okay—let's go for it!

- First read the story and make sure that:
  - all the events in your plot are in order and that you haven't left anything out.
  - the reader will know where and when the story is taking place, which ought to happen pretty early in the story, hopefully in that first, attention-grabbing sentence. In our sample story, you'd want to change this:

    Amanda had just moved to Brooklyn and it was almost dark and she was sitting on the front porch.

    To this:

    That summer evening as Amanda sank into the front porch swing, she decided that she hated this town of Brooklyn for sure. "It's 1951," she thought to herself. "And everybody else is having a wonderful time—but here I am in a place where everybody hates me."
  - the reader can really picture your main character and his or her problem character. Look for those physical and personality traits you planned, as well as the main character's problem. Make sure you've SHOWN those things, rather than just told them. In our sample story, you would change this:

    Amanda had straight blonde hair. She pushed it behind her ears when she was nervous.

    To this:

    Amanda pushed her own blonde hair behind her ears as she watched Betty's dark curls bounce when she walked importantly across the street as if she owned it.
- Now work on adding dimension to your story. You know what a noun is—person, place, or thing. Go through your story and circle the nouns. Now go back and make sure the reader can SEE each of those nouns just the way you do in your mind. Can you add color, shape,

size, type, or other details? Could a "bicycle" be a "red girl's bike with shiny silver handlebars"?

- You know what a verb is—an action word. Go through your story and underline the verbs. Now go back and make sure the reader can SEE each of those actions the way you do in your imagination. Can you find specific verbs to replace plain ones—like "flopped down onto the porch swing" rather than just "sat on the porch swing"?
- Finally, read through your story and make sure it's exactly the way you want it. If you think one word might sound better than another, try it. If you want to show more of your main character's feelings, you do that. You're the boss.
- If you really like it, now is the time to get some help with the spelling and punctuation and usage and then produce a clean, correct-as-you-can-make-it copy. By now it's a work of art that belongs to you, so you might want to make a cover for it or even illustrate it. Send it to your grandmother or stick it on the refrigerator with a magnet or ask the whole family to listen to you read it out loud. You've done something pretty complicated, my friend. Congratulations.

Seventh/Eighth: What you've written is your rough draft. That means you have the important stuff down, but you'll want to polish it up. This part is like putting the clips in your hair after you've washed, conditioned, dried, and curled—or like trying some behind-the-back, under-the-leg shots after you've learned the basic set shot. Let it be fun by following this process. (And by the way, since this is a ROUGH draft, scratch things out as you need to, scrunch things between the lines, draw arrows to the margins to put stuff in. The messier the better, because it means you're really working on your story.) Okay—let's go for it!

- First read the story and make sure that:
  - all the events in your plot are in order and that you haven't left anything out.

- the reader will know where and when the story is taking place, which ought to happen pretty early in the story, hopefully in that first, attention-grabbing sentence. In our sample story, you'd want to avoid sentences like *Bubbles was a clown living during the depression in Cleveland, Ohio, in a dingy basement.*

- the reader can really picture your protagonist and his or her antagonist. Look for those physical and personality traits you planned, as well as the protagonist's problem and the antagonist's weak spot. Make sure you've SHOWN those things, rather than just told them. And reveal as much as you can early on so there are no unfair surprises for the reader. In our sample story, you would change this:

  Warm, loving Bubbles, who was tall and thin, had a landlord who was greedy and had a pencil-thin moustache.

  To this:

  Bubbles' tall, lanky form lurched a little as he crossed his apartment to open the door for his landlord. Mr. Wheedle stood in the doorway, stroking his pencil-thin moustache with one bony hand and holding the other one out with the fingers beckoning for money. Money Bubbles didn't have.

• Now work on adding dimension to your story. Make sure the reader can SEE each noun the way you do in your mind, adding color, shape, size, type, or other details. (Instead of "a basement apartment", make it "a gray basement apartment with cold walls and cobwebs on its only window, which he shared with a family of rats.") Make sure the reader can SEE each of your verbs the way you do in your imagination, finding specific verbs to replace plain ones (like "teetered for a horrible second above the roof before crashing through" instead of simply "stopped over the roof and then fell through"). Make sure you've included at least one of your other senses besides sight in the story—fit in a description of a sound, a smell, a taste, or a touch detail.

- Look for emotions and/or thoughts in your story, both experienced by your protagonist and described in your antagonist. If there are none, include them now. If there are, make sure the reader will be able to feel or understand the thoughts of the character just as you do. "Bubbles felt his heart sink nearly to his toes as he read the notice, and his shoulders sagged," will work better than, "Bubbles was really disappointed."

- Finally, read through your story and make sure it's exactly the way you want it. If you think one word might sound better than another, try it. If you want to make your antagonist even more evil, make it happen. It's your story, born in your imagination, so you're the boss.

- If you really like it, now is the time to get some help with the spelling and punctuation and usage and then produce a clean, correct-as-you-can-make-it copy. By now it's a work of art that belongs to you, so you might want to make a cover for it or even illustrate it. Send it to your grandmother or stick it on the refrigerator with a magnet or ask the whole family to listen to you read it out loud. You've done something pretty complicated, my friend. Congratulations.

Christianity Folder

In this folder, I've provided the themes from each book that you might explore in discussions, writing activities, or projects such as the ones suggested in other folders. The chapter numbers given will guide you to the spots where the themes are most specifically dealt with. I'll be praying for you.

The Discovery

Christian Theme: Keeping the faith can sometimes be hard. It's tough to keep something so abstract a conscious thing. It's tempting to feel embarrassed by it. When times are really tough, it can seem almost impossible. The only way to hang on to faith is to let God help. We all have to learn to let Him help us untangle ourselves! One way is to learn from other wise Christians who have seen the mystery of the way God works. No matter how much we mess up in the faith-keeping business, God still believes in us—so much so, in fact, that He gave us Jesus to show us the path to follow. We begin by simply praying.

Focus Chapters: 1, 15, 18, 19

The Mirage

Christian Theme: God still works miracles. People who remain strong and faithful will experience them in their lives. Sometimes staying faithful means asking God tough questions—like why He lets bad things happen. If we are to remain in faith and experience God's miracles, we need to seek Him—by praying, expecting our prayers to be answered, expecting God to do what only God can do, listening for His instructions, and paying attention, because God can work through anybody or anything. We have to remember, though, that God sees things differently than we do. But when He works things out the way they're supposed to be—*that's* a miracle.

Focus Chapters: 3, 5, 6, 9, 11 ,12, 13, 14, 15, 16, 17, 21

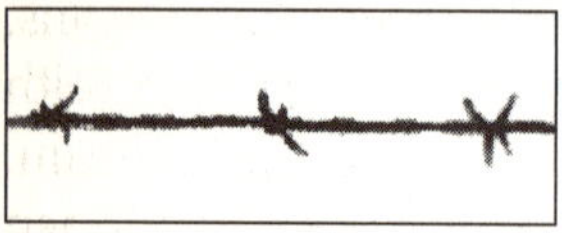

The Stand

Christian Theme: God wants us to look for common ground with people. That means talking to God a lot to know what that common ground is. We have to remember that the bottom line is "God is love," not "God is hate." We also need to be forewarned that it can sometimes be lonely, because certain people we attempt to find commonality with will turn away. And there is room for a certain kind of hate: we sometimes have to hate what people have done with what God has made, but we must never hate the people themselves.

Focus Chapters: 2, 3, 6, 9, 10, 11, 13, 15, 16, 17, 18

The Mission

Christian Theme: We absolutely have to pray if we are to stay connected to our God. But the answers to those prayers are up to God. We have to accept them with faith. Sometimes we get disappointed, feeling as if we can't count on God, feeling like it doesn't matter that God loves us. But if we have a good foundation with God, He won't let us feel that way for long. If we keep praying in spite of our doubts and disappointments, God will lead us to a point of understanding. Then we have only to follow.

Focus Chapters: 2, 5, 7, 8, 9, 11, 12, 13, 14, 15, 16, 17

The Struggle

Christian Theme: Turning the other cheek—loving our enemies and praying for those who hate us—can be very hard. It can seem as if there is no fight we can win. However, there are some battles we *can* fight, and God gives us the freedom to choose. The ones we can't fight we have to surrender to God—which is what turning the other cheek means. God doesn't expect us not to have any bad feelings; it's what we do with them that counts. The first thing to do is take those feelings to Him. At that point, He teaches us what things He won't negotiate on. When we're young it's important to learn that we cannot always have what we want in life, because as we get older, fewer people put limits on us. Basically, we have to learn to fight the battles against things that are hurting God and His people. We're still going to need God's help in the fray—and we have to have faith that it will be there.

Focus Chapters: 3, 4, 5, 7, 12, 13, 14, 15, 16, 17, 18

The Choice

Christian Theme: Our choices *do* matter. We just have to look to God to help us make the right ones, and the ones He makes for us we have to accept. Sometimes it's hard to know the difference between God's choices and ours, but He can even help us with that part, and for that help we need to pray. Once we know, we can then concentrate on the choices we *do* have. Sometimes God will help us to know the right decisions through other people, sometimes through circumstances, and sometimes through His Holy Spirit speaking to our heart. One of the best ways is to consider what Jesus would do—and the Bible helps us with that and, again, so does talking to God and being in silence with Him. After all, Jesus walked with His people and showed them how to live on earth. It isn't a guessing game! Other choice-issues dealt with in Book 6 include questioning other people's choices, what to do when we make the wrong choice, sharing our choices with the people who will be affected by them, being patient while waiting for God to show us the right choice, and what to do when a choice is taken away. Two choices we must always make: (1) to make sure everyone has the freedom to choose and serve God; and (2) to trust God in all things.

Focus Chapters: 1, 3, 5, 6, 7, 9, 10, 11, 12, 13, 14, 15, 16, 17, 18, 19

Ways-to-Make-It-Matter Folder

These are ideas for putting it all together once you've completed the entire series. I recommend you have your students select only one activity. Don't let my choices limit you!

Third/Fourth:

- Remember Will taking out the box of family pictures? Create that "box of pictures"—full of the characters in The Santa Fe Years. Include both the fictional characters and actual people (like General Eisenhower, etc.). You can use your own drawings or photocopies of pictures from books and old magazines. Be sure to identify the people in the pictures. Then decorate your picture box 1940s style!
- When Will's dad gets home (Book 6), there's so much to tell him that Will looks through his scrapbook to make sure he doesn't miss anything. Imagine that you're in Will's position. Make a scrapbook, poster, or shadowbox to capture important events. (Examples: a turquoise pin, his letter from Uncle Al, or a program from the Stars Over America Cavalcade.)

Fifth/Sixth:

- Remember how in Book 1, Will's assignment was to do a report on his ancestors? He tried to substitute "Growing Up Indian," and had to redo the whole project. Create the report Will finally did, writing about what you've learned about Will's family and the Hutchinson background and what they're all about (there are lots of hints at the end of Book 6!). Be as creative as you can.
- Remember in Book 5 when Will and Miguel teamed up to do a three-dimensional project for the "Treasures of New Mexico" assignment? You be Will (team up with a partner if you can) and create a three-dimensional project that represents "The Challenges of Growing Up During World War II". Review all you've learned about the problems of being on the home front as a kid, and then create a diorama or storyboard to represent those problems. Make it as 1940s as you can!

Seventh/Eighth:

- Will kept a scrapbook of World War II events in the Pacific theater. Choose a theater—Pacific or European—and put together a scrapbook that follows the war as it unfolded there. You might be able to find actual newspaper clippings in books that you can photocopy; others you may have to write yourself. You can draw pictures, make charts, include maps—anything you want.
- Will is a very different boy at the end of Book 6 than he was at the beginning of Book 1. Create a timeline that shows the changes in Will as they happened through The Santa Fe Years. Illustrate it. Show ups and downs. Be specific. Include the people who influenced him along the way, perhaps including pictures or drawings of them at appropriate places above the timeline. Then create a timeline that shows how YOU have changed over the last year and a half of YOUR life. You might need your parents to help you with that part—or if you keep a journal, use that as your guide.

Feel-Free-to-Photocopy Folder

Don't hesitate to put the following pages into your copy machine and crank out as many as you like (enlarge them if you can) for your own use. The top left corner of each sheet will tell you for which subject and grade level the exercise is intended and to which book it's related.

History/*The Discovery*
Third/Fourth

What Did Will Learn…

about going to school in Santa Fe? Name three things:

____

____

____

about life as an Indian on a pueblo? Name three things:

____

____

____

about ways kids could make money for the war? Name one thing:

____

about things that were rationed during the war? Name two things:

____

____

History/*The Discovery*
Fifth/Sixth

Culture Shock!

Will found life in Santa Fe very different from the kind of life he'd had before. If he were to put together a booklet called *A Guide for Anglos Moving into Santa Fe*, what would he put in each of these sections?

Two things to know about the way classrooms are run (when you've always been homeschooled):

____

____

What to expect being an Anglo (white person) among so many Hispanics. Name two things:

____

____

One building to use as a landmark when lost: ________________

Two things about the way many Hispanics conduct themselves which may be hard to adjust to at first:

____

____

Two things about the way the Indians conduct themselves which may seem strange or different at first:

____

____

History/*The Discovery*
Seventh/Eighth

Scrapbook Headlines

If you were going to make a scrapbook about the events in the war like Will did, what are some articles you would have included at this point? (You'll know this from what you've read in *The Discovery*.) Write just the headlines below.

History/*The Mirage*
Third/Fourth

Beware!

The rationing of everyday items during the war caused Americans on the home front to make adjustments in their lifestyles. Using the things Will and his mom and Fawn had to use carefully and change in their daily lives, fill in the blank posters below with three of those, as if you are actually warning people to be very careful.

History/*The Mirage*
Fifth/Sixth

Imprisoned!

You've learned some things about prisoners of war in this book—some very hard things. Write them on the horizontal bars of the jail windows below.

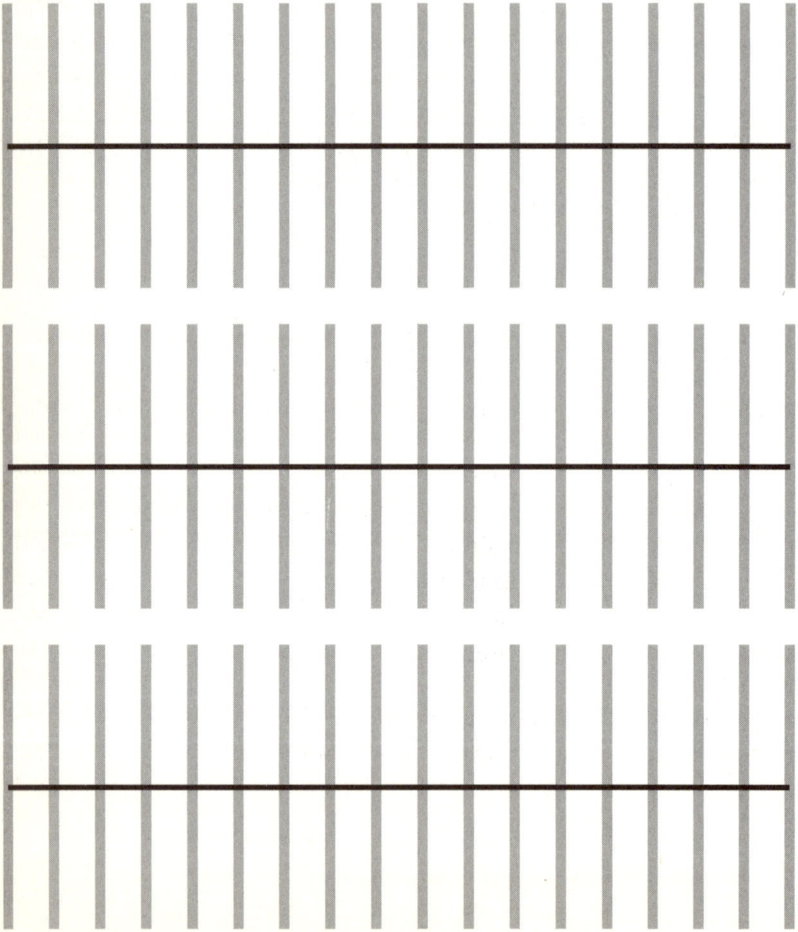

History/*The Mirage*
Seventh/Eighth

Discrimination!

First look up the word *discrimination* in the dictionary if you don't already know what it means, and write the definition here:

____

Now imagine that you are going to present to the judge a complaint about discrimination going on in Santa Fe and in the country as a whole at this time in World War II. List the complaints—as you find them in *The Mirage*—on the "official" document below:

Official Complaint Against Discrimination

-
-
-
-

History/*The Stand*
Third/Fourth

Closed In

On each of the pieces of barbed wire below, write one thing you now know about Japanese internment camps.

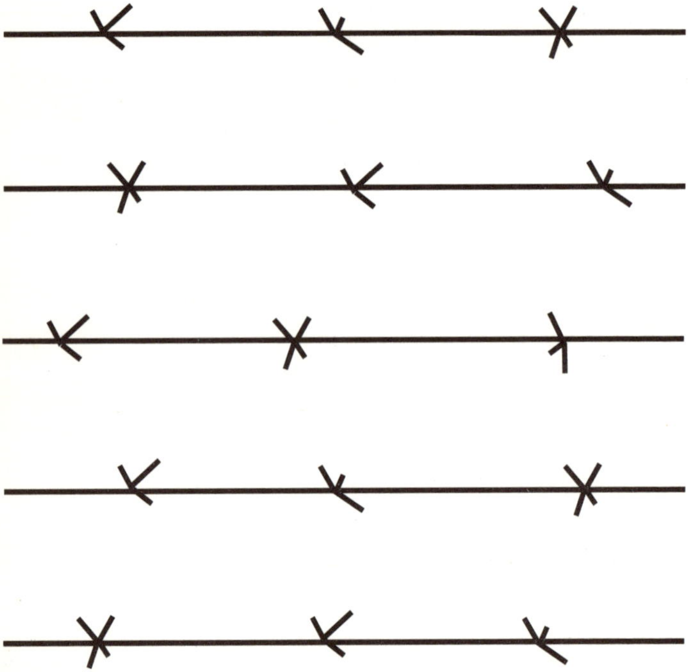

History/*The Stand*
Fifth/Sixth

Are They Speaking a Foreign Language?

Several terms with which you might not be familiar are used in the book, and if you're going to understand the history in the story you have to know the language. Fill in our dictionary below with definitions in your own words, if you can, or even the way Will would say it.

History/*The Stand*
Seventh/Eighth

To the Rescue

If you were going to help a Japanese family get out of a relocation camp, such as the ones the Lins were in, you would need to have your act together. Fill in the following:

Written plan for their employment, schooling, and living quarters

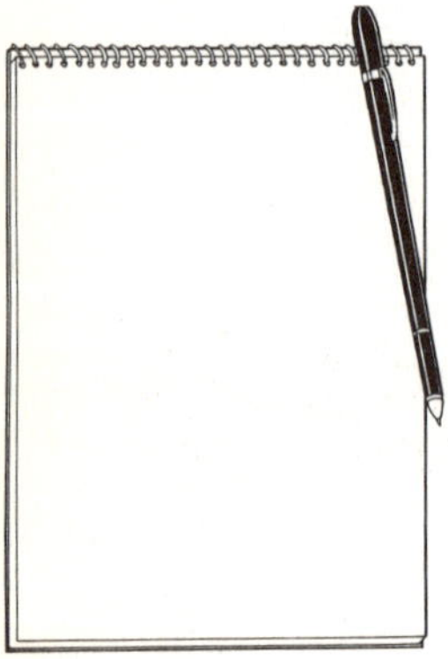

A leaflet asking people to donate money to help the family

The protest sign you're going to need when people oppose what you're doing and try to keep the family out of such places as schools and restaurants

History/*The Mission*
Third/Fourth

Gifts!

It's the gift-giving season in this book. What are three gifts that a kid living at home with a dad fighting or being held prisoner or missing because of the war would have liked to have received in 1944? The first "gift" has been done for you as an example.

A telegram from Dad

History/*The Mission*
Fifth/Sixth

The Learning Goes On—In and Out of School

Will is in school part of the time in this book, and the other part he's on Christmas vacation, but the entire time he's learning. What does he learn about the war and the home-front effort from each of these "textbooks":

The theater usher (see p. 5)

____

____

The Stars Over America Cavalcade show (see p. 26)

____

____

Mom's report of her conversation with Uncle Al (see pp. 15-16)

____

____

Fawn's letter from her father (see pp. 79-80)

____

____

Will's conversation with Uncle Al (see pp. 86-87)

____

____

History/*The Mission*
Seventh/Eighth

There Are Going to Be Some Changes Made

As you found out in this book, there were big changes for a lot of people on the home front because of the war. Write a statement in each box, written as if you, the reporter, were quoting a spokesperson for that group of people.

Indians Fighting
in the War

Prisoners of War as
the War Progressed

Hispanics Who Had to Abandon
their Lives in Small Towns

History/*The Struggle*
Third/Fourth

Hand It Over!

As you know now from reading this book, kids on the home front had to make a lot of sacrifices (give up things) because of the war. On each of the hands below, write one sacrifice a kid (or anybody) had to make:

History/*The Struggle*
Fifth/Sixth

Going Downhill

By the time you get to this book, you see that the longer the war went on, the harder things became on the home front. On the downward slope of the hill below, list three examples of things that were NOT going well on the home front:

1.

2.

3.

History/*The Struggle*
Seventh/Eighth

Define…

To really understand what was happening at this point in the war, both overseas and on the home front, you need to make sure you know the terms involved. Fill in our dictionary page below with definitions for:

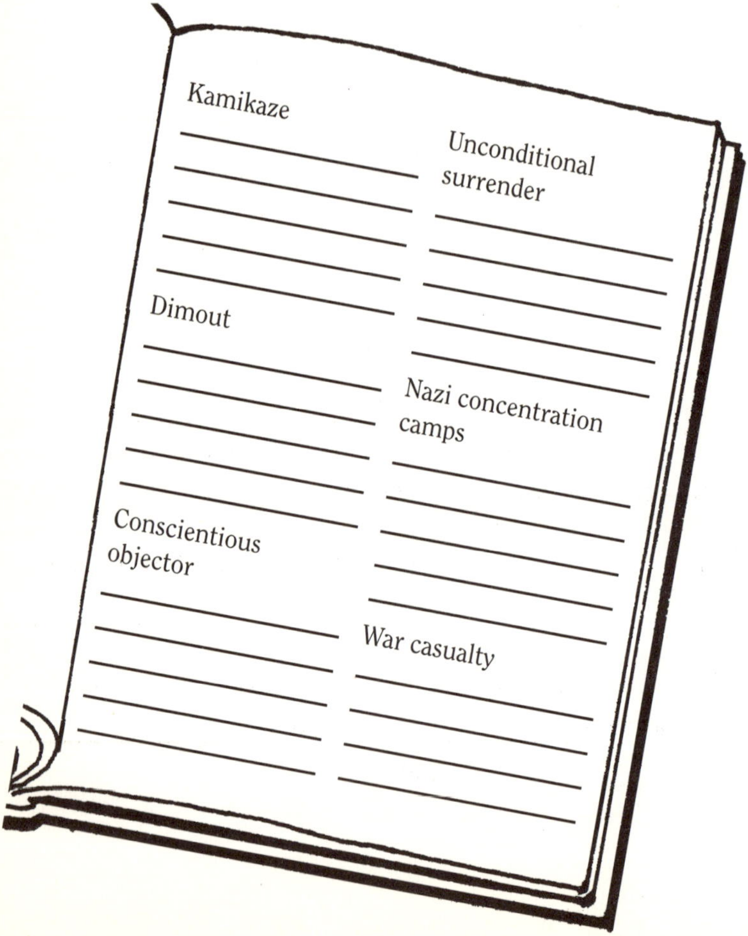

History/*The Choice*
Third/Fourth

Now You Know the *Rest* of the Story

To make sure you understand all that was going on in history during this book, fill in the blanks below with the terms given:

Navajo Code Talkers	Nagasaki
unconditional surrender	Bataan
atomic	rationing
Hiroshima	

The only way the Allies would agree that the war was over would be if Japan would agree to an ______________________________.

When the war was over, American soldiers found the prisoners of war who had been held at ______________________________.

Indians like Fawn's father served as ________________________ to help keep the enemy from knowing what the Allies were talking about as they sent messages to one another.

On the home front, people were still having to limit their use of things like sugar because of food ________________________.

Finally, it seemed the only way for the Allies to get the Japanese to surrender was to drop ___________ bombs over ______________ and ______________, Japan.

History/*The Choice*
Fifth/Sixth

They Were There

Match these made-up characters from the book with the real-life relationships they had with the war.

Rudy Hutchinson	Served with the American Red Cross
Dan McHorse	Served in a Special Intelligence Unit
Uncle Al	Was a conscientious objector
Aunt Hildy Helen	Was a prisoner of war
Eduardo Fernandez	Was a Navajo Code Talker

History/*The Choice*
Seventh/Eighth

Look What War Did...

The things soldiers and others had to go through during the war definitely affected them personally, and the characters in this book reflect that. Fill in the "Reports" below with what you know about the changes in each of these characters as a result of involvement in the war, keeping in mind that those same changes actually happened in real people.

Report on John Daniel McHorse	Report on Hildegarde Helen Hutchinson	Report on Rudolph Hutchinson

Literature/Plot
The Discovery
Third/Fourth

Discover the Mistakes

Which of the following things happened in *The Discovery*, and which didn't? Put an X next to those that didn't take place, and write what actually DID occur on the line provided underneath.

_____ Will Hutchinson started at a new school, and even though he had never actually gone to a public school before, he fit right in.

____

_____ Will figured the best way to make friends was to win the war stamp contest—but to do that, he ended up having to lie about some things—and then one lie led to another.

____

_____ Will and his mom got a telegram from his father, telling them that he was okay and was being treated well.

____

_____ Will stole some money out of Margretta Dietrich's purse to buy enough war stamps to win the contest.

____

Literature/Plot
The Discovery
Fifth/Sixth

Discovering Why

It's important in a story for events to "make sense." That means that there has to be a reason for everything that happens, and everything that happens has to result in something else happening. It's called CAUSE AND EFFECT.

Listed below are some causes of events from *The Discovery*. For each CAUSE, list the EFFECT it had.

CAUSE	EFFECT
When Will felt like a misfit at school, and then Miss Ortiz announced the War stamp contest...	
In Chapter Three, Will wasn't paying attention while he was riding his bike to school, so...	
The first day Will met Fawn, she asked him about a hundred questions, so he...	
Will's mom had never told him he was adopted, so when he found out, he...	
Will didn't really know who he was now, so when he went to the Pueblo...	

Literature/Plot
The Discovery
Seventh/Eighth

The Plot Thickens

I. This is the way the plot in *The Discovery* is constructed (which may be a review for those of you who have used the other guides).

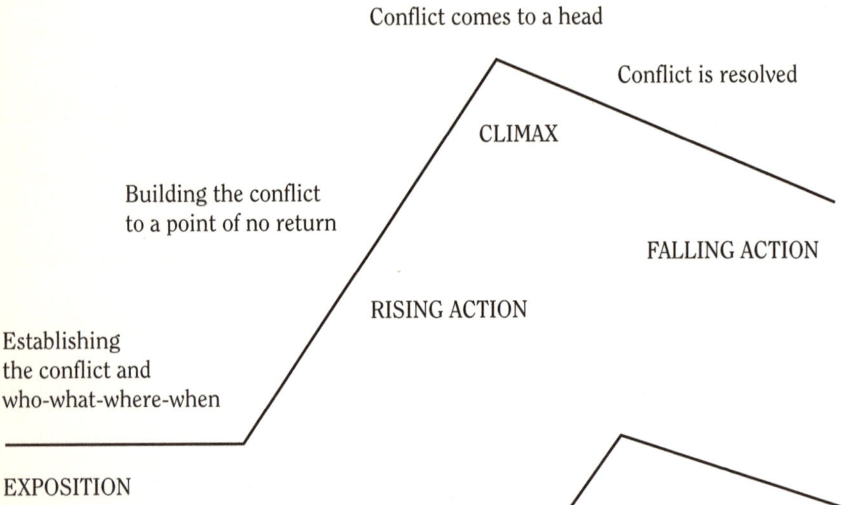

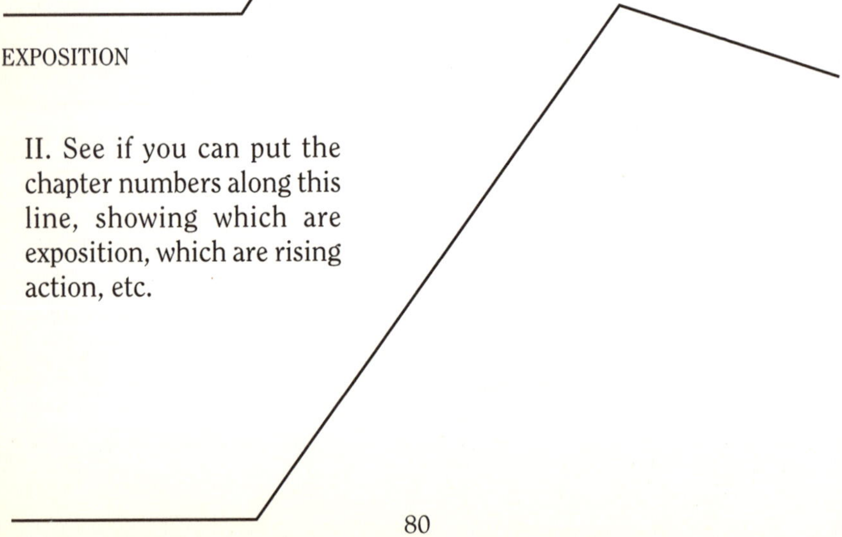

II. See if you can put the chapter numbers along this line, showing which are exposition, which are rising action, etc.

Literature/Characters
The Mirage
Third/Fourth

Let Me Tell You a Little about Myself

In your literature activity for this book, you're going to choose two of the characters that you like the most in *The Mirage* and have those characters each write a letter to the other one (or a telegram if you're just getting started in writing), telling about themselves. This sheet will help you prepare to do that.

Pick your two characters from the book and write their names here. Then in the space below each character's name write the answers to the questions about each character:

	____________________ (character 1)	____________________ (character 2)
1. boy or girl?		
2. adult or kid?		
3. what race?		
4. biggest desire?		
5. main interest?		
6. main weakness?		
7. best feature?		
8. goals?		
9. fears?		
10. faith in God?		

Literature/Characters
The Mirage
Fifth/Sixth

Why Can't Everybody Just Get Along?

Make a list of 10 of the characters in *The Mirage* on the lines at the left.

Decide whether each character really works out problems, or either doesn't address the problems or continues to handle them the wrong way. Put a check in the YES column if he or she does work them out, and put a check in the NO column if he or she doesn't. Now, in the WHY? column, write why you think that person does or doesn't work out problems. You can keep you answers very simple, such as "listens to adults" or "doesn't seem to know anything about God."

	YES	NO	WHY?
____________	___	___	________________________
____________	___	___	________________________
____________	___	___	________________________
____________	___	___	________________________
____________	___	___	________________________
____________	___	___	________________________
____________	___	___	________________________
____________	___	___	________________________
____________	___	___	________________________
____________	___	___	________________________

Literature/Characters
The Mirage
Seventh/Eighth

Good Guys and Bad Guys

The following are character terms that people who discuss literature use so they can understand one another. Each term is defined for you. Write in the blank provided the name of a character or characters who fit that term.

Protagonist: The main character through whose eyes you are seeing the story. This is "the good guy," that you root for.

____

Antagonist(s): The person or people who make it very difficult for the protagonist to reach a goal or to fulfill a main desire. The antagonist is ALWAYS against the protagonist. There can be more than one antagonist, so there are three lines provided. You don't have to fill them all.

__________ __________ __________

Secondary Characters: These are people who support either the protagonist or the antagonist(s) in a major way. They sometimes argue with the protagonist but usually remain on his/her side. There are several important secondary characters in this book, so several lines are provided, but don't worry if you don't fill them all.

__________ __________ __________ __________ __________

Minor Characters: These are people who serve a brief purpose and then they're gone. There are several of those in this book, so several lines are provided. Once again, don't let it bug you if you don't fill them all.

__________ __________ __________

Literature/Historical Fiction
The Stand
Third/Fourth

Come On—What *Really* Happened?

The Stand (and all of the Christian Heritage Series books) are historical fiction, which means they use real facts as their background, but the characters and the things that happen to them are made-up—fiction.

Below are some things you'll find in *The Stand*. Decide whether each one is HISTORICAL FACT or HISTORICAL FICTION and put a check mark in the right column. All of the FICTION did happen in the book—you're just looking for the difference between FICTION and HISTORICAL FACT.

	FACT	FICTION
Will Hutchinson's father was a prisoner of war.	_____	_____
People in the U.S. during World War II had to use ration coupons to buy things like sugar, shoes, gas, and meat.	_____	_____
The Allies in the Pacific slowly took back the islands that Japan had conquered.	_____	_____
Luis and his friends really gave Will a hard time.	_____	_____
Japanese-Americans were kept in camps during the war.	_____	_____
Fawn and Will hid two Japanese kids in their basement.	_____	_____
Will led a "strike" against the school board for not letting Kenichi go to public school.	_____	_____
The army let some people leave the camps and go and fight in the war.	_____	_____
FBI Agent Graves helped make people see what Kenichi's rights were.	_____	_____

Literature/Historical Fiction
The Stand
Fifth/Sixth and Seventh/Eighth

Mixing It Up—Without Getting Mixed Up!

Below are some passages from *The Stand*. They are partly fiction and partly historical fact. Below each one, write the fact or facts that have been woven into the fiction.

1. "With his (Will's) father probably a prisoner of war in the Pacific somewhere, and Fawn's father serving in Europe…and both of Abe's original Jewish parents maybe dead or in some German camp set up by Hitler—Will took a deep breath from just thinking about all of it."

---

2. "Mr. DeWitt tossed his match aside and pumped furiously at the new cigar before he took it out to speak. 'That relocation camp,' he said. 'The one just outside of town.' He motioned with his cigar. 'They're set up all over the west—Colorado, Arizona, Utah, you name it.'"

---

3. "It was hard for Will to believe that his father wasn't still out there fighting, especially in 1943 when the American soldiers and their Allies had fought their way up the necklace of South Pacific islands Will pointed out to Abe on the map."

---

4. "Emi said, 'Our dad's in the army—he's overseas somewhere.' Will's heart sped up. 'Which army?' 'The U.S. Army!' Kenichi said. "What do you think?' 'But I don't get it,' Will said. 'They let a Japanese fight in our army?' 'It's our army, too!' Kenichi said. 'He's a Nisei—that's a person with Japanese parents born in America.'"

Literature/Theme
The Mission
Third/Fourth

Boy, Has *He* Changed!

If you can figure out how a main character changes, you'll know what the author wants you to learn.

What is Will like in the very first chapter? How is he coping with his father still being away in the war?

____

When Will finds out that his father was not one of the rescued prisoners—that God didn't answer his prayer the way he wanted Him to—how did his thinking change from Chapter One? (for help see p. 52)

____

What happens to make Will realize that he's wrong about his new approach? (for help see p. 139)

____

What does he do that proves he isn't using that way of dealing with things anymore? (for help see p. 139)

____

What has Will learned by the end of the story? ____________

____

Literature/Theme
The Mission
Fifth/Sixth and Seventh/Eighth

Get a Clue, Will!

Will made a number of mistakes in the book, but the way he solved them really shows us what the author (that's me!) wants YOU, the reader, to know and understand. Below you'll find a list of Will's mistakes. Beside each one, write what action his mistake in thinking led him to do.

Will thought that just because he prayed to God for a particular thing, God was going to give him exactly what he asked for. ____________________

Will thought the secret mission up to Chimayo was going to make him feel like he was actually doing something for his father—because God obviously wasn't doing anything. ____________________

When Will had to go to the pueblo instead of meeting Miguel, he didn't tell his mom. ____________________

Finally Will realizes he's been wrong about God and he learns a huge lesson, which is:

____

Then he takes some action to make right the things he's done wrong, using the lesson he's learned. Describe that action:

____

Literature/Setting
The Struggle
Third/Fourth

Two Different Worlds

The place where Olive lives is very different from where Will makes his home. Describe both of those places using the key words on the left to guide you.

	WILL'S PLACE	OLIVE'S PLACE
Location		
Yard		
Comfort		
Beauty		
Cleanliness		

Literature/Setting
The Struggle
Fifth/Sixth

I Can Just *See* It!

If the author (that's me!) has done her job well (and we HOPE so!), she has painted word pictures for you so you can actually see the setting. Below are some page numbers with settings. Next to each, write down the words that create a picture of each setting in your mind.

Page 3—the Plaza

Page 13—Canyon Road

Page 19 of Chapter Two—Mr. T.'s house

Page 41 of Chapter Four—the desert where they rode horses

Page 137 of Chapter Fourteen—Olive's house

Literature/Setting
The Struggle
Seventh/Eighth

What Difference Does It Make?

Would it matter if *The Struggle* were set in a different time and place? Decide by thinking about each of these events in the book and figuring out whether the place or the time period (World War II) is vital to the scene. Check the appropriate box if it does seem to be vital. Sometimes you will check off both boxes.

Chapter One: Will and his friends are collecting waste paper for the war effort and get into a fight with a store owner who thinks it's a waste of time. ____TIME PERIOD ____ PLACE

Chapter Five: Because of the shortage of meat during the war, some people took to cattle rustling, and Mr. Tarantino's cows were stolen from his ranch. ____TIME PERIOD ____ PLACE

Chapter Eight: Will fell into a turquoise mine shaft.
____TIME PERIOD ____ PLACE

Chapter Fourteen: Olive's father was a conscientious objector so he and Olive lived in seclusion out in the desert hills.
____TIME PERIOD ____ PLACE

Looking now at your check marks, decide whether the setting of this book is important to the story, or whether it could have happened at any other time and in any other place.

SETTING MATTERS _____

SETTING DOESN'T REALLY MATTER _____

Writing/Story Ideas
The Discovery
Third/Fourth

What a Great Idea!

Ideas for historical fiction stories (or ANY stories!) can come from just about anywhere. Let's just look at a few that are available to you right now.

Below several story idea sources (where they came from) are listed. Below that are some story ideas. Write the ideas under the sources you think they came from. This will give you a chance to "play" with the idea. (Some ideas may fall under more than one source).

SOCIAL STUDIES BOOKS

NONFICTION BOOKS

TALKING TO ADULTS

STORY IDEAS:
A story about a young dinosaur
A story about a kid whose father died in the war
A story about the Battle of the Bulge
A story about a train conductor during the Civil War
A story based on your great-grandfather's experience in World War II
A story about raising the flag at Iwo Jima

Writing/Story Ideas
The Discovery
Fifth/Sixth

Why Didn't I Think of That?

You CAN! Just use the sources that are available to you right now. Below are five of those sources, and under each one are three possible ideas. Circle the one that looks like the best idea to you.

YOUR SOCIAL STUDIES BOOK
- A story about the Battle of the Bulge
- A story about what happened the first day of the Battle of the Bulge
- A story about a scared young soldier on the first day of the Battle

YOUR SCIENCE BOOK
- A story about the very moment penicillin was discovered
- A story about the boy sweeping the lab the moment penicillin was discovered
- A story about the discovery of penicillin

YOUR FAVORITE NONFICTION BOOK
- A story about a boy who FOUND a dinosaur bone
- A story about dinosaurs
- A story about collecting dinosaur models

TODAY'S NEWSPAPER
- A story about a family's house being robbed while they're away
- A story about the robbery of a house
- A story about robbery

AN INTERVIEW WITH AN ADULT
- A story about what it's like to be a fireman
- A story about a fire station
- A story about what it's like for a fireman to be a rookie at his first fire

Writing/Story Ideas
The Discovery
Seventh/Eighth

Whose Idea Was This, Anyway?

It could be YOURS! Below are five sources, and under each one are three possible ideas. Circle the one that looks like the best idea to you.

ANY OF YOUR SCHOOL BOOKS
- A story about algebra
- A story about solving equations
- A story about a kid who can't do algebra and considers cheating

ANY NONFICTION BOOK YOU'VE READ
- A story about a kid traveling to France
- A story about a kid traveling to Valence, France, and getting lost
- A story about French travel

A NEWSPAPER OR MAGAZINE
- A story about a boy arrested for selling drugs who swears he's been set up
- A story about drugs
- A story about a boy arrested for selling drugs

OBSERVATIONS MADE WHILE SITTING IN AN AIRPORT
- A story about a lady who's obviously afraid to fly
- A story about a teenage couple who have a baby
- A story about a kid who looks like he can't wait to get on the plane

Writing/Characters
The Mirage
Third/Fourth

Now *That's* an Interesting Character

I bet you can figure out what makes a character interesting to read about, just by doing the exercise below.

First, decide which one of these characters would be the most interesting for someone to read about and put a check mark in front of that character:

_____ A 10-year-old boy who lives with both parents, loves school, has a lot of friends, and is really good at sports

_____ A 10-year-old girl who lives with both parents and gets along fine at home. She has trouble fitting in at school because she still likes to play, and all the other girls are into boys and makeup

Now decide which one of these characters would be the most interesting for someone to read about and put a check mark in front of that character:

_____ A 10-year-old who is jealous of the fact that the other kids have more money and gets back at them by talking behind their backs

_____ A 10-year-old who gets along with absolutely everybody

Do you know now what makes a character interesting? See if you can fill in the blank below:

For a character to be interesting, he or she has to have a _______________.

Writing/Characters
The Mirage
Fifth/Sixth

What Makes You Take a Second Look?

See if you can figure out what makes a character interesting just by doing this exercise.

Which of these physical characteristics would make a character interesting? Circle as many as you want to.

bright red hair/ mouse-brown hair/ a nice nose/ dreamy blue eyes

tall for his age/ average height/ freckles all over/ pale skin

Which of these personality traits would make a character interesting? Circle as many as you want to.

cries at the drop of a hat/ is always cool, calm, and collected

is really funny/ is so serious it's kind of strange/ is never serious

loves to do things spontaneously/ always goes along with the crowd

Which of these characters would be more interesting for someone to read about? Put a check mark next to that character.

______ A 12-year-old who has a great family life that everybody envies and is loved by all teachers and friends

______ A 12-year-old who has a great family but has issues with a teacher because he teaches things that go against the 12-year-old's beliefs

An interesting character has to have clear physical characteristics, unique personality traits, and a ______________________________.

Writing/Characters
The Mirage
Seventh/Eighth

Unforgettable

See if you can figure out what makes a character interesting just by doing this exercise.

First, do the sheet on the previous page for the Fifth/Sixth grades.

Now, choose the character below that YOU find interesting. Put a check mark next to it.

_____ A kid who spends the summer working in a gold mine in California and actually finds some gold—only no one will believe him/her because our character has told some real whoppers before in trying to be accepted

_____ A kid who has been in a successful movie. When he or she returns to school, everyone treats him or her differently and it's hard to be just a normal kid anymore

Now, in the space below your character, write a description of a character who would be a friend to our character. Don't fill up the whole space.

In the rest of the space below your character, write a description of a character who would give our main character trouble. Be specific.

Writing/Creating Setting
The Stand
Third/Fourth

This Is a Great Place!

One of the most fun parts of writing a story is picking out where and when it's going to take place. The possibilities are endless because YOU'RE in charge! However, no generic settings allowed!

Let's practice with that. Below are some *places* for a story. Check the ones that are NOT generic. HINT: There are three.

_____ a house by a lake in Michigan

_____ somebody's house

_____ on a street

_____ at the lion's cage at the zoo

_____ at an antique car show in Hershey, PA

Let's do the same with *times* for a story. Check the ones that are NOT generic. HINT: There are three.

_____ one morning

_____ the summer of 1968

_____ the night before the start of the Civil War

_____ anytime is fine for the story

_____ one brisk winter morning in 1814

Writing/Creating Setting
The Stand
Fifth/Sixth

Ready on the Set?

It's important to create a setting for your story that is specific. We need to know at least these things—and probably more:

town state season year

From there you can fill in more details, such as a specific house, a time of day—that kind of thing.

Let's see if you've got the idea. (You probably do—it isn't rocket science!) Three of these five settings below are specific enough for an interesting story. Check those three off.

_____ early winter in Tennessee, at sunset on the lake where all the trees are bare

_____ one summer on a beach

_____ in a big house a long time ago

_____ a summer afternoon on the island of Maui, just last year

_____ early fall; a mountain cabin up in the Blue Ridge Mountains

Here is a main setting for a story. See if you can come up with settings for two scenes within the story . They need to be specific and they need to fit within the main setting.

MAIN SETTING: A run-down neighborhood of Chicago. It's the middle of summer, so the heat is sweltering. Present day.

SPECIFIC SCENE SETTING #1: ____________________

SPECIFIC SCENE SETTING #2: ____________________

Writing/Creating Setting
The Stand
Seventh/Eighth

Imagine the Scene...

From the other exercises we've done, you've probably figured out that the more specific the time and place of your story are, the more interesting it's going to be to the reader. So obviously, SETTING #1 below is not as interesting as SETTING #2.

Setting #1—a backyard in summer in a suburb

Setting #2—a perfectly manicured backyard in suburban Atlanta; mid-summer; two large oak trees hold up a green-and-white-striped hammock

In the spaces provided below, see what you can do with describing in more specific detail each of these generic settings:

- A castle in ruins in France. It's spring in the present time.

- A foggy day in the city or town you live in—about five years ago

Writing/Building Plot
The Mission
Third/Fourth

There Is a Plot Afoot

The easiest way to build a plot is to follow this simple plan:

- give your character a problem
- make that problem worse
- make the problem even worse
- finally, let the character solve it

Give it a try. Here's a problem. Make it worse, even worse, and then decide how the poor character is going to solve it.

PROBLEM: A girl wants to be accepted by a certain group that always hangs out together on the playground, but they make fun of her because she stutters big-time.

MAKE IT WORSE: ______________________________

MAKE IT EVEN WORSE: ______________________________

HOW WILL THE CHARACTER SOLVE THE PROBLEM?: __________
____

Writing/Building Plot
The Mission
Fifth/Sixth

A Plot Has Been Hatched

The easiest way to build a plot is to follow this simple plan:

- give your character a problem
- make that problem worse, using the setting to give you ideas
- make the problem even worse, again using the setting to give you ideas and perhaps changing the scene within the setting
- finally, let the character solve it

Try your hand at one.

PROBLEM: A boy in New York City dreams of being an actor and one day in January (present time) has a chance to audition for a part in a commercial. But after bringing it up at the dinner table in their high-rise apartment, our character's parents won't let him because they think the acting world is a dangerous place for a 12 year old.

PROBLEM GETS WORSE,
POSSIBLY IN A DIFFERENT SCENE SETTING:

PROBLEM GETS EVEN WORSE,
POSSIBLY IN A DIFFERENT SCENE SETTING:

PROBLEM IS SOLVED,
POSSIBLY IN A DIFFERENT SCENE SETTING:

Writing/Building Plot
The Mission
Seventh/Eighth

Just When You Thought Things Couldn't Get Worse...

To build a plot that's interesting and fun to write, follow this plan:

- give your character a problem that involves the antagonist
- make that problem worse, using the setting to give you ideas; this might involve the antagonist, though the main character may make things worse, perhaps with a friend's help
- make the problem even worse, again using the setting to give you ideas and perhaps changing the scene within the main setting; the antagonist should be involved somehow
- finally, let the character solve it

Now try your hand at it.

PROBLEM: A homeless boy lives in a shelter in Philadelphia. It's Christmas time and he wants to buy his best friend, who also lives in the shelter, a gift. He has no money. The director of the shelter is always accusing the boy of things he didn't do.

PROBLEM GETS WORSE BECAUSE OF THE SHELTER DIRECTOR:

PROBLEM GETS EVEN WORSE BECAUSE OF THE SOLUTION OUR CHARACTER AND HIS FRIEND TRY:

CHARACTER SOLVES THE PROBLEM:

Writing/Starting to Write Your Story
The Struggle
Third/Fourth

Ready...Set...Go!

Now that you have your story basically planned out, you can start writing. Try this easy starter plan.

In your first two sentences, show the reader these three pieces of information:

- the main character
- the setting
- the main character's problem

CHARACTER, SETTING, and PROBLEM: a kid in a store who is a genius with computers wants a Game Boy but he doesn't have enough money.

POSSIBLE FIRST TWO SENTENCES: Marcus stood in the middle of the aisle at Electronics R Us, staring at the Game Boy he didn't have the money for. He so wanted to go at that Game Boy with his computer-genius mind.

Now you try it.

CHARACTER, SETTING and PROBLEM: a girl wants to be accepted by a certain group that always hangs out together on the school playground, but they make fun of her because she stutters big-time.

FIRST TWO SENTENCES:

Writing/Starting to Write Your Story
The Struggle
Fifth/Sixth

One Sentence at a Time...

Now that you have your story basically planned out, you can start writing. There's an easy way to jump-start yourself. Once you get going, the rest won't be so hard (and "the rest" is explained in the **Writing Folder**).

In your first two sentences, show the reader these three pieces of information:

- the main character
- the setting
- the main character's problem

CHARACTER, PROBLEM, SETTING: A girl on a soccer team in a small town (present day). Other kids on the team are planning to cheat at the next game. Our character knows she should tell the coach, but that would get all her friends mad.

POSSIBLE FIRST TWO SENTENCES: Marcy stared down at her knees as the other girls on the soccer team sat in the circle with her on the grass, plotting their moves for the next game. She didn't utter a word, because she knew what they'd say if she told them she hated cheating and dirty playing on the field—and it wouldn't be pretty.

Write the first two sentences from this situation:

CHARACTER, PROBLEM, SETTING: A boy in New York City dreams of being an actor and one day in January (present time) has a chance to audition for a part in a commercial. But when he brings it up at the dinner table in their high-rise apartment, our character's parents won't let him because they think the acting world is a dangerous place for a 12 year old.

Writing/Starting to Write Your Story
The Struggle
Seventh/Eighth

Time to Go for It

Now that you have your story basically planned out, you can start writing. There's an easy way to get launched. Once you get going, the rest won't be so hard (and "the rest" is explained in the **Writing Folder**).

In your first two sentences, show the reader these four pieces of information:

- the main character
- the setting
- the main character's problem
- the antagonist who is eventually going to make that problem worse

CHARACTER, SETTING, PROBLEM, ANTAGONIST: A homeless kid living in a shelter in Philadelphia. It's Christmas, and the kid would like to buy his best friend in the shelter a gift. Of course, he has no money. The director of the shelter is always accusing him of things he didn't do.

POSSIBLE FIRST TWO SENTENCES: Jason sat glumly on his mattress pallet, cold and keenly aware that he had no money in his pockets to buy Angela so much as a candy cane, which a person could use in this un-Christmasy place. What a person could do without was Old Man Riker, who was currently making his way across the cement floor with the usual suspicious look on his face, probably ready to remind Jason that he was nothing but a homeless punk and had better not be up to something.

Now you try it.

CHARACTER, SETTING, PROBLEM, ANTAGONIST: a 14-year-old girl going on a hike with a youth group up a mountain in the Rockies. She is scared to death of heights but doesn't want to look like a wimp. A bully in the group catches onto her fear right away and starts milking it for all it's worth.

YOUR FIRST TWO SENTENCES:

Writing/Polishing It Up
The Choice
Third/Fourth

Here's Where It Gets *Really* Fun

At this point, if you've been working in the **Writing Folder**, your rough draft is all done. Pat yourself on the back—you've done something really complex. Now let's work on polishing it up.

It's always better to SHOW the reader rather than just TELL the reader things. Here are some examples. Once you have the idea, you fill in the rest of the SHOWS column:

TELLS	SHOWS
Jeff was 10 years old and had some pretty big ears.	Jeff looked in the mirror at his 10-year-old face and shuddered at the sight of his ears. He was sure that if he wagged his head back and forth, they would flap.
Lizzie got mad.	Lizzie could feel her face turning red and clenched her fists. She really wanted to use those fists to pop Emily Warner right in the nose.
Adam felt like he was going to throw up.	Adam could feel his lunch churning in his stomach. He was sure that any minute now it would be heading for his throat.

TELLS	SHOWS
Kristen was pretty.	
Ben had the biggest feet in the class.	
Hannah was afraid of snakes.	
Luke hated math.	
Kate got along really well with her mother.	
Even at eight years old, Kevin tried to live the way Jesus taught.	
Lester was really popular.	

Writing/Polishing It Up
The Choice
Fifth/Sixth

This Is the Fun Part

At this point, if you've been working in the **Writing Folder**, your rough draft is all done. You go, girl—or boy. You've done something really complex. Now let's polish it up. I'll lead you through some ways to do that.

- Be sure that when you've described your *setting*, you've SHOWN, rather than simply TOLD. "Show, Don't Tell" is a common writing rule. Here is an example. Once you see how it works, you fill in one.

TELLS	SHOWS
It was a run-down house.	It was impossible to get up the steps of the house because their rotten boards had been broken through a long time ago. Every window was jagged with busted glass, and the roof looked as if it were going to cave in any minute.
It was a desert.	

- Do the same with introducing a character and his/her problem.

TELLS	SHOWS
He was 14 and he liked going to church, only he was afraid to tell the guys on the basketball team because they'd make fun of him.	The walk to the church was through a neighborhood with sidewalks and manicured lawns, but Joe kept looking anxiously over his shoulder as if there were gangs lurking behind the hedges. He just wanted to make sure none of the guys from the basketball team saw where he was headed. He could just hear Andrew Bagly now, saying, "I didn't know you were a Jesus Freak."
A 13-year-old kid has a great singing voice but also a bad acne problem, which is keeping him or her from performing in public.	

Writing/Polishing It Up
The Choice
Seventh/Eighth

Now *That's* What I'm Talkin' About!

At this point, if you've been working in the **Writing Folder**, your rough draft is all done. Be impressed with yourself—you've done something really complex. Now let's work on polishing it up. I'll lead you through some ways to do that.

First, do the worksheet for the Fifth/Sixth grades on the previous page.

You, as a seventh- or eighth-grader, can take it even further, making it even more interesting to read. The trick is to look at certain kinds of words and make sure they're specific. Study the examples below and when you think you've got it, try the fill-in.

- Look at your nouns and be sure the reader can see it the way you do.

OKAY	DEFINITELY BETTER
Car	A red '64 Mustang souped up with shiny chrome and a stereo that makes other drivers vibrate in their cars.
Dog	

- Look at your verbs and be sure they show the exact action you want to portray.

He walked down the street.	He took the sidewalk in long strides, swinging his arms confidently at his sides.

- Try to include the other four senses in addition to sight as often as you can without overloading your story. Go ahead and go big, and if it sounds too overdone, you can always cut later. It's part of the process.

HEARING

There was an explosion.	A thunderous sound boomed from the warehouse and roared in his ears.
He heard an airplane go over.	

SMELL

There was a disgusting odor.	The stench of garbage made her pinch her nostrils together. That bag of trash had to contain rotten fish.
She smelled good.	

TASTE/TOUCH

It was yucky.	The egg was so runny, she spit it into her napkin. There was nothing nastier than the feel of slimy yoke oozing in her mouth.
She liked ice cream.	